TO: _Darcy_

FROM: _Barb Goodrow_

DATE: _2-10-18_

Sarah Andrus

WOMEN WHO RIDE
REBEL SOULS, GOLDEN HEARTS, AND IRON HORSES

SARAH ANDREAS

Sarah Andreas

Published by WiseWood, LLC.

9246 State Route 250 NW, Strasburg, Ohio 44680 USA
© Copyright 2018 by Sarah Andreas. All Rights Reserved.
Email: author@womenwhoridebook.com • Subject Line: Women Who Ride
Visit our websites:
www.wisewoodllc.com
www.womenwhoridebook.com

Disclaimer: This is not an official publication from any of the motorcycle manufacturers mentioned in this book. The motorcycles named by brand name in this publication, as well as certain names, models, designations, are the property of the motorcycle manufacturers. In this publication they are used for identification purposes only. Neither the author, photographers, publisher, nor this book are in any way affiliated with the manufacturers referenced in this book.

This is not an official publication from any of the dealerships mentioned in this book. The names of the dealerships are the property of the dealership. In the stories in this publication they are used for identification purposes only. Neither the author, photographers, publisher, nor this book are in any way affiliated with the dealerships referenced in this book.

Would you like to share a story in our next publication?
Send contributions to author@womenwhoridebook.com

Library of Congress Control Number: 2017918243
ISBN-13: 978-0-9983303-2-7 (WiseWood, LLC)

Andreas, Sarah
True stories by, for, and about women with Rebel Souls, Golden Hearts and Iron Horses/Sarah Andreas
1. Inspiration 2. Recreational 3. Self-Help

DEDICATION & ACKNOWLEDGMENTS

DEDICATION

Dan, thank-you for your support and love.
Marcus, I love that you give me my own lectures back. It makes me laugh!

ACKNOWLEDGMENTS

Thank-you to Sheryl Roush for her encouragement and guidance through this process!

To the women who ride and made this book possible.
This book is wonderful because of you!

CONTENTS

FOREWORD

You've probably had more than one of "those" kinds of meetings. The ones where a friend of yours connects you with a friend of theirs because they know the two of you are possibly a good match based on what they know about you both. Such was the case when a mutual powerhouse friend, we'll call her Sheryl Roush, because that is her name, tagged me in a Facebook post, with a woman we'll call Sarah Andreas, because well, yep, you guessed it, that is her name. Sarah had posted a request for stories of "women who ride" motorcycles. Sarah wanted these stories for this very book you are reading. Our mutual friend Sheryl knew "Oh, yeah, June has stories from 12 years of riding!" Sheryl and I go back at least 20 years as both of us are professional speakers, authors, and coaches. Sheryl is a well-respected, all round awesome woman and a great connector. So, after her third, okay, maybe forth tag, I thought "Dang it, I'd better slow down long enough to reach out to this riding chick before I bump into Sheryl at some speaker meeting and have to say… "No, Sheryl, I never did connect with your riding friend, what was her name?" Have you, like me, found guilt and shame to be a powerful motivator? There's therapy for that and it may be time for me to make an appointment.

But, oh my gosh, am I ever so very glad I did slow down and private messaged Sarah midafternoon on a Monday. That began an awesome dialogue about her book project celebrating and inspiring women who ride. Her passion was palpable as she spoke of the three main sections of her book: Rebel Souls; Golden Hearts; and Iron Horses, which are filled with women's personal riding stories from all across the globe. They share their journeys and the courage it takes to ride. Talk about inspirational. "Do you have room for one more story," I asked

Sarah hopefully as I suddenly realized I DO NOT want to
NOT be a part of this woman's dream and vision. "Yes," she
replied. Whew! Thank goodness I finally did slow down enough
to make this connection! Our friend Sheryl was so right because
quite frankly, Sarah had me at "women who ride."

Flash forward a couple of weeks when Sarah private
messaged me, "June, I know you were thinking about writing a
story for my book, BUT" (in a millisecond my brain skidded to
a screeching halt—just like those back bike brakes can
sometimes do as I thought uh-oh! She doesn't want or maybe
doesn't need my story now, Double Bummer!), she continued,
"would you be willing to write the foreword for my book?" My
brain did a gee-haw in the opposite direction and took off like a
skittish filly, "WHAT?" I thought to myself, "you don't even
know me and I don't know you," as I typed back, "When can
we talk?" It took a couple of days for our busy schedules to
match up for our second EVER phone conversation. I
poignantly asked, "Sarah, why do you want ME to write the
foreword for your book?" "Well," she began, it was an easy
decision. Two things about you make you the perfect person to
write this. One, you are 'THE' self-proclaimed Southern, Sassy
and Savvy Harley-Riding Humorist. AND, you did a GREAT
Facebook video about not being too old for denim. You
encouraged and inspired people to go for the very dream they
had maybe given up as you told how late in life it was when
your dream to ride your own Harley came true at age 53. You
told us to stop limiting ourselves, to do, be and live OUR
amazing lives. You told us we were not too old for denim…not
our dreams. That's why you are the perfect person to write the
foreword for my book."

Whoa and Wow! So, now my brain said "This is a
BRILLIANT WOMAN and instantly erased my original

thought of, "Does this woman not have any friends?" Of, course, she has friends. But, do you know what? We already were friends, soul friends, riding sister kind of friends. The kind of friends you meet for the first time and know you have known them forever. Because of our shared passion to ride, the courage it takes and the freedom it brings, we know each other better than many friends know each other in a lifetime. In fact, passion, courage and freedom are just some of the common traits that bond the sisterhood of women riders. It's also the message woven in the personal stories you will find on these pages of the three powerful sections of "Women Who Ride." Of course, I am "the perfect person" to write this Foreword. Not only did I have to, I wanted to. I am honored to. I can feel the inspiration of each of these women from all over the world. In fact, it gives my goose bumps, goose bumps which I call *Angel Hugs.* I believe...no, I know you will feel these stories. They will touch your soul. These "Women Who Ride" will become "those" kind of friends. Let me know if your goose bumps get goose bumps. When you do, you've been hugged by an Angel who rides.

My new soul sister riding friend, Sarah, asked me to share one of my humorous stories with you here. There are so many I actually created a one-woman show called, "Make It a Great Ride," with all of my crazy stories. One of my most painfully vivid was the time I finally had the courage to ride my 883 Custom Deluxe Harley-Davidson Sportster I named "Good Golly Ms. Molly" on the Interstate. I lived in Tempe, Arizona and the interstate nearest to my home was called 'the 60.' I had been riding for less than 6 months but only on the residential roads near my house. To say my learning to ride was a challenge would be--kind. I was even named "most likely NOT to succeed" by my motorcycle riding class. That day, I "felt" it. It was time. I remember being both terrified and exhilarated riding down that ramp gaining speed and merging beautifully with traffic. I clung to Good Golly Ms. Molly for dear life totally frozen, focused, my hands locked on to the handle bars staring straight ahead to where I wanted to go. Cars were passing me and suddenly, I noticed some of the people in them were waving at me. Of course, I could not wave back… I knew I would die. Then I noticed some passengers were pointing. Some were laughing, giving double thumbs up. Some were even clapping and I remember thinking, "WOW! How nice! LOVE their support! But, how do they know it's my first time on the interstate?" I had driven at least two or three miles when I finally felt comfortable enough to flash a glance down to check my speed. I was going 60 on the 60! It was AWESOME and the fastest I had ever been on Good Golly Ms. Molly. YAY! But in that same nano-second glance, I noticed something white fluttering under my chin. What? My tucked in shirt had come un-tucked and was flapping wildly about chin and my armpits. I was flashing belly, boob and bra riding down the 60. In my total panic of overexposing myself, I dang near crashed. I learned a valuable lesson that day. You can NOT re-tuck a shirt going 60 down the 60.

No wonder folks were going crazy and waving like they were being picked for a game show. I was giving them quite the show. I took my show on the road and took it off the interstate at the very next exit, re-tucked myself and took the back roads home. Though I thought I would die from embarrassment, I did live to ride 'the 60' a thousand other times …wearing spandex tank tops from that fateful summer day forward. Spandex is your friend…it stays tucked in! That's my story and just one of my idiot moments on a motorcycle. Gosh, I have so many more. Sometimes you don't know what you don't know...until you know.

What I know now is it's time for you to get 'tucked' in with your favorite libation in your favorite chair in comfy clothes. Prepare to relax and for your life to be touched by "Women Who Ride" with Rebel Souls, Golden Hearts and Iron Horses. Be prepared to snicker, laugh, guffaw, sweat a little around the eyes and to feel some tugs and Angel Hugs of the heart. My hope is that you are inspired by their stories, that their courage builds your courage that you grant yourself the freedom to go for it AND that you know you are never too old for denim. My hope is that you are empowered by the new soul sister riding friends you will meet on these pages and that they become 'those' kind of friends. The kind that you are blessed to have, like our good friend Sheryl Roush who connects kindred souls. Thank you, Sheryl. You did good.

And finally, to my new soul sister riding friend, Sarah Andreas, I am so glad I slowed down and connected with you. What an amazing accomplishment, contribution and labor of love you have created here. Thank you for acknowledging us. You honor me with your asking me to write this Foreword I was destined to write. Here's to you, my new friend, and to all "Women Who Ride."

ENJOY these journeys and always...Make It A Great Ride!

For more videos, views and content from June Cline, contact her at: www.JuneCline.com, https://www.facebook.com/JuneCline2 or https://www.facebook.com/loljunecline or via email June@junecline.com

INTRODUCTION

"As soon as I saw you, I knew an adventure was about to happen."
— Winnie the Pooh

I knew this book was going to be an adventure from the first moment the idea to write it popped into my head. I have heard for years that when you find your passion, the world starts to align. I have found that to be true. Ten years ago, I took the leap to learn how to ride a motorcycle and I have fallen in love with the experience. I was scared and unsure but determined to succeed. I have dropped my bike several times, gotten lost, found myself and embraced the journey. It is not, however, just the riding that I have fallen in love with...It is the women who ride. They have this beautiful camaraderie that is hard to find anywhere else. They come together to ride and nothing matters about their personal lives except the fact that they ride. The grandma, businesswoman, the housewife, political parties, makeup or no makeup...the dividing lines seem to melt away in the presence of their love for the sport of motorcycling.

This book is dedicated to all the women who have taken their passion for riding and turned it into this beautiful relationship with their motorcycles and the other women who ride. Riding seems to bring the balance that we need in our lives. It brings peace, satisfaction and a sense of accomplishment. Over the past ten years, I have seen women who ride donate generously of their time and money to support great causes while riding. I have seen a woman stop what she was doing to help encourage a new rider to pick her bike up and get back on. I have experienced their willingness to share their "been there done that" stories that encourage the woman who dropped her bike to have the determination to get back on and ride. I have also seen them have the courage to stand up for what they believe is right and hold their own against family, friends, and acquaintances that try to discourage them from riding a motorcycle.

Many of my contributing co-authors have similar stories. The core message of this book is to celebrate women who have rebel souls, golden hearts and iron horses. Their courage reminds me of Marianne Williamson's writing about our deepest fear:

Our deepest fear is not that we are inadequate.
Our deepest fear is that we are powerful beyond measure.
It is our light, not our darkness that most frightens us.
Your playing small does not serve the world.
There is nothing enlightened about shrinking
so that other people won't feel insecure around you.
We are all meant to shine as children do.
It's not just in some of us; it is in everyone.
And as we let our own lights shine, we unconsciously give
other people permission to do the same. As we are liberated
from our own fear, our presence automatically liberates others.

The last two lines are what I believe each woman who contributed to this book is doing. She is letting her light shine and giving others permission to do the same. Facing her fears. Liberating others. I hope that the stories we share will inspire you to ride or remind you of the love for riding.

Embrace the journey,
Sarah Andreas

REBEL SOULS

"It takes courage to grow up and become who you really are."
— *E.E. Cummings*

FREE YOUR REBEL SOUL

My story began as a 12-year-old child riding a 125 Yamaha all through the creeks and pastures on the farm where I grew up in Kansas. I loved the freedom of the outdoors and the wind in my face though I always had to wear a helmet, even then. I continued to ride that dirt bike even into my high school years and would often ride the dirt roads to school. Of course, I was the only girl who did this. Other girls wore makeup and had perfect hairdos but I did not care about that for myself. I had always been a bit of a loner, but my guy thought my riding was great.

Fast-forward to my early 20's and married life. Before children, my husband and I would ride a 750 Yamaha and later an 1100 Yamaha on many wonderful trips through the Colorado Mountains. I was a passenger at that time. Then the children came and the bike had to be sold, but we vowed that when the children got older we would each have a bike and keep riding. Well, that just didn't happen as life doesn't go according to our plans often times.

Fast-forward 30 years. I was 55 years old. We had raised good kids and even had grandkids. My husband and I had great paying jobs and were financially comfortable. But I needed something more. I was longing for the freedom of the road and riding again. But my husband had so many hobbies of his own being an avid hunter and fisherman that he didn't have time to spend with me riding. Plus over the years we had been growing in different directions and were often "miles apart" literally. I had never spent the money or carved out time for myself like he had. I knew I had to do this for myself.

I approached him about buying a Harley for myself. And like several times before over the recent years, he was adamantly against it. But this time I didn't give in. This time, at the age of

2

55, I fought hard. He'd said I had no business riding a big bike at my age and that I wouldn't be able to handle it and would get killed. His words hurt but I believe he was genuinely worried about my safety. Plus he was happy with me just being home while he enjoyed his hobbies. But I needed the adventure, the challenge and something to feel passionate about again. My last words of the fight were telling him that I was doing this with or without him. The next day he called to say "go ahead if that's what you need."

I immediately signed up for the MSA course at a junior college approximately 2 hours away. I had many second thoughts since I wasn't getting emotional support at home or from my adult kids. I didn't know any other women who rode at that time so I did a lot of soul-searching and praying. The book study part was easy for me, but the riding was not. We practiced on a 350 Suzuki. I hadn't ridden myself since my dirt bike days as a teen. I was struggling to get up to the speed the instructors wanted and ride through a curve. At my highest point of frustration, as I waited my turn to ride the curve again, I prayed.

"Jesus, I thought we were good with this. If it's really okay for me to do this Lord, please, please help me. Show me a sign."

It was a hot day in the middle of a large vacant parking lot at the college. Just then a small breeze blew a beautiful yellow feather across the pavement in front of me. I took that as my sign and dug deep for more determination and passed the riding skills test with no problem! There! Take that husband of mine. But he still told me I wouldn't be able to handle a big Harley. That only fueled my fire and the rebel in me said just watch me.

A short time later he went on a week-long fishing trip. I went to the local Harley-Davidson dealership and bought my first bike, a Harley-Davidson Super Glide Custom. The crazy thing was that after sitting on the bikes I was very intimidated by the size and weight of them and honestly felt scared. Very scared. The salesman tried and tried to get me to test ride different bikes but I knew if I did, I would scare myself and back away and never make the purchase. So I bought the bike and rode it home cold turkey.

Again, my doubts crept in and my praying continued.

"Oh my, what have I done? I've never spent this much money on myself. What if I can't do it?"

I rode my first 3,000 miles all by myself so I could get comfortable with less distraction. I dropped it twice during that time and picked it up by myself being thankful I'd watched videos on the correct way to do that. After 8 months, I continued to struggle with the bike feeling top-heavy especially when coming to a stop and at slow speeds in parking lots. Now with a few miles and some confidence, test riding a Harley-Davidson Heritage Softail was the perfect solution for that. I traded in my Super Glide Custom for the Heritage Softail that same day.

Soon after purchasing the Heritage, I joined the local H.O.G. chapter (Harley Owners Group) and they took me in under their wings. I met so many nice people who offered encouragement. They praised me for following my desire to ride even without my spouse. Every ride out got a little bit easier and my confidence grew. My parents offered great support as they had ridden through almost every state in the U.S. Only 11 months after buying my first Harley I had already traded for a bigger one and had ridden the Million Dollar Highway in Colorado. I'd found what I was looking for and more! I was in love with the wind. Finally, 18 months after I started riding, my husband bought a bike and we began growing closer in our marriage! WIN – WIN!

In the past four years I've owned 3 bikes. I currently ride a 2016 Heritage Softail and have ridden 32,000 miles. My husband and I have had many great trips together riding. We just celebrated our 40th wedding anniversary and are closer than ever.

Follow your dreams, ladies, even if you have to fight for them. I can't express enough the feelings of joy, freedom, empowerment, independence, and confidence I've gained in riding. Be true to yourself and RIDE ON REBEL SOULS!

– Barbara "Barbie" Goodrow, is currently riding a 2016 Harley-Davidson Heritage Softail

Meet Barbie Goodrow, a 59-year-old medical professional who has worked 35+ years as an x-ray and ultrasound technologist. She currently works part-time and watches her grandson three days a week. She is a mother to a son and a daughter, and grandmother to two granddaughters and one grandson. Her current ride is a 2016 Harley-Davidson Heritage Softail and dearly loves the cruise control after riding her first 23,000 miles without it.

FINDING COURAGE

"Embrace the calling of your Rebel Soul...
You never know when it will stop asking you to follow your true
path" – Sarah Andreas

Too many people in the world push their rebel souls so far down that it takes immense effort to get it to reemerge. It's sad because they have passion and are destined to be great artists, singers, dancers, doctors, lawyers, and motorcycle riders. But they try so hard to fit the cultures in which they were raised and don't honor the people they should become. We all have something great that we are meant to do in our lives. Taking the time to rekindle your rebel soul and find your fire can help you rediscover this great destiny. Find the rebel soul that dreams about riding a motorcycle across the country. The soul that dreams of art and painting, of singing and dancing, of going back to college. Whatever your rebel soul dreams of, let it free! We are here for a short time and there is no guarantee we will have the strength, ability, or power to do it tomorrow. This section celebrates the women with Rebel Souls.
– Sarah Andreas

SADIE GRIMM – A REBEL SOUL FROM HISTORY

One of our contributors is a gentleman named David Rupps. David sent me this email after hearing the interview about my book on the *Motorcycle and Misfits* podcast. This is what he wrote...

Sarah, I have a story you might be interested in. In 1914, a motorcyclist named Sadie Grimm (How bad ass is her name!). She rode in a cross-country race from Winnipeg, Manitoba, Canada to the town of Winnipeg Beach, on her Indian Big Twin. At 19, she won and was the first person to ride a bike to the town and first woman in Canada to win a race open to men.

There were no roads to Winnipeg Beach, she rode through pastures, swamps and down railway tracks. Not a huge deal by today's standards, but when put into 1914 context, bike with little suspension, no cell phones or any way of contacting anyone if she got hurt or broke down, etc. ... Really cool!!

I'm not an expert on her, I just discovered her this past summer, but I would like to share a quote from her published July 1914:

"My trips on a motorcycle have been one long list of pleasures. In the first place, the motorcycle is a great teacher... it teaches one to be more dependent on herself, to know with a twist of the wrist she can control the powerful little machine that will carry her swiftly and safely wherever she wants to go. I don't think anyone could recommend a better doctor than nature... On the two-wheeler, one can take a spin into the country after working hours in the evening or early in the morning and Sundays and holidays can be spent entirely out of doors." – Sadie Grimm, 1914

Meet David Rupps. He is a 1965 model year biker currently living in Canada. He has two daughters, Chloe and Stacey. Who are both in their mid-20's. David says they don't ride yet but he is encouraging them to take it up and when they do he will be there for them 110%. David did not do any serious riding until 2012 when he got his motorcycle license and he has not been off the bike since. He currently owns seven motorcycles that are all mid 70's Honda's except for a 1950 Triumph. David's go-to, is a 74 cb550 that he hardtailed with several other models. He says, "It's my bagger... I love it and take it everywhere." David reports that the one ride he looks forward to the most is the one with both the girls, whatever that will be. He can't wait.

DREAMS DON'T ALWAYS COME TRUE, BUT SOMETIMES THEY TAKE YOU ON A GREAT RIDE.

We all have dreams. Some come true, and some just remain dreams. A long time ago when I was about eight or ten years old, my dream was to be a motorcycle stunt woman. I know that sounds crazy, but that was the era of Evel Knievel jumping over trucks and busses in his red, white, and sparkly blue outfit. A motorcycle stunt woman sounded like an exciting career, and I could envision myself performing stunts in action movies. One day in the mid 60's I was with my dad at a place that sold lawn mowers, and I saw my first motorized two-wheeler. That mini-bike was love at first sight. It cost a hundred dollars, which was a fortune at the time, but I saved for over a year and dreamed every night that the mini-bike would be mine.

It was no secret that I was obsessed with saving for my dream. My older brother Ken would ask me every few weeks how much I had saved. In the late summer of the second year, I had only saved $80. I will always remember that day because he reached into his pocket and gave me the last $20 I needed! I couldn't wait until Saturday came and my dad brought me over to buy that mini-bike. I had a lot of fun on that bike over the next few summers. What I remember most, was the way I felt when I was riding. I was no longer a child burdened by school obligations; I was a motorcycle stunt woman! I guess that feeling stuck with me even when I outgrew the mini-bike and bought my first motorcycle, an SL350 Honda. It was a used dirt/street combination motorcycle with a sparkly turquoise tank. It didn't quite match my stars and stripes helmet, but I didn't care. When I rode that bike, I was no longer a socially awkward, minimum wage factory worker. Although I wasn't doing motorcycle stunts, there was no better feeling than kick-starting that bike and rolling on the throttle as I shifted through the gears. Sadly, we get caught up in the norms and obligations of life, and I sold my Honda and focused on family, college, and a career. I don't regret those choices. It was a time when other dreams took over my life and time passed quickly. During that time I experienced both the good and bad of life: children, career, divorce, and death of loved ones. And then one day something really strange happened. I remembered that feeling of the wind on my face, the excitement of riding on two wheels and rolling on the throttle. I wanted that feeling of confidence and power again. It wasn't easy, but I finally convinced myself that anything is possible if you want it bad enough. I hadn't ridden a motorcycle for thirty plus years, so I decided to take a motorcycle safety class, which was invaluable. Then I met my boyfriend who loves to ride motorcycles. He helped me pick out my 750 Harley Street and insisted I buy good boots and protective gear. We have been riding together for a little over three years now. The best part of the experience is that every time I ride, I leave behind the stress of my daily life. When I get on my motorcycle I become a different person; I feel confident and powerful. Although not confident enough to start jumping buses, I enjoy the feeling of pressing the bike into a turn and rolling on the throttle.

One day this summer I was riding down a country road when I saw this girl, about eight or ten years old riding a sparkly purple scooter. She zipped down her driveway and turned onto the shoulder of the road. As I saw her approach, she rolled on the throttle and gave me the biggest smile. I nodded to her as I passed, and couldn't help but smile. I have since thought about her and wondered about her dream. Maybe she is Wonder Woman or Batgirl. Whoever she is, I bet she feels confident and powerful. I hope she carries that feeling with her throughout life and grows up with the confidence to take a risk and question status quo. Maybe she will be the one that makes a big discovery that will improve all our lives. Just maybe, she is Wonder Woman after all.

– Dr. Donna Matteson, she rides a 750 Harley Street

*Meet Dr. **Donna Matteson** from New York. She is a College Professor for the School of Education, Department of Technology Specialty: Architecture, CAD, and 3D Printing. Her hobbies include traveling, riding motorcycles, Jetski, painting, and spending time with her grandkids.*

WILL THE REAL BAD-ASS PLEASE STAND UP?

"Less really is more; more encounters, more freedom, more places, more fun. The simplicity of just riding." -Michelle Robart

Since high school, I've been fascinated with those carefree rebels who ride motorcycles. A friend and I used to sit on the couple of bikes that were parked in our school parking lot in the spring, pretending we were one of those rebels. My fascination with motorcycles never left but life got in the way, I joined the military, married, raised a family, served my country overseas...Fast- forward 30 years later. After 20 years I retired from the military and landed a job in the oil and gas industry. A co-worker rode to work, and we got talking about bikes and how to get a license. I suggested to my husband that we take the motorcycle safety course just to try it, neither of us had ever ridden a motorcycle, and on the premise that we didn't like it, it gets struck off my bucket list. We took the course in May 2012, and by August we both had our license and had purchased a couple of Suzuki Boulevards as starter bikes. I loved it. The freedom and confidence it gave me was incredible, it opened a whole new world, not to mention I felt like a bad-ass. I ride a 2007 M50 Suzuki Boulevard – how bad-ass is that! Well, apparently, not that bad-ass as I was about to find out a few years later.

In the summer of 2015, we moved our daughter out to Halifax, Nova Scotia to attend University. During our week on the East Coast, my family took in the Digby Wharf Rat Rally, the largest motorcycle rally in Atlantic Canada. It was our first rally, but because we flew out to Nova Scotia, we didn't have our bikes, so we admired all the other incredible bikes that were there and hung out with like-minded people from all over the country.

A few days later, back in Halifax we made a trip to the laundromat. While waiting for the laundry, the rest of the family went to look for a printer for my daughter. It was sweltering hot, and people were milling around outside the shop. As I sat on the step, I noticed two Harleys. Nice bikes, I thought to myself. Then out came two guys and they went to sit on the two Harleys - obviously waiting for their laundry. One thing I found with "bikers" is that it doesn't seem to matter who you are or what you do for a living, we just all love riding. So, because of that common thread, striking up a conversation with people who are different than you is quite normal. That is what I truly love about the biking community. Everyone belongs. Young, old, rich, poor, professionals, laborers, women, men, moms, dads, gang members. Yes, unbeknownst to me; gang members. Before riding, I would have never approached someone as intimidating as a guy wearing all leathers, tatted and patched. It's different now, all those tattoos, leathers, and patches don't intimidate me. So not even thinking twice, I mentioned to them both they had nice bikes, and that my husband and I rode as well and asked if they took in the Wharf Rat Rally. It turns out they did and were on their way back to Ontario. We chatted about the Rally, how far it takes them to travel from Ontario to Nova Scotia and just idle chit-chat. The conversation turned interesting when they mentioned how the Hell's Angels do such great work, how much money they raise for charity and one of the guys dazzled me with incredible dollar figures the club has raised for charity over the years. Looking back, I'm not even sure how we got on the Hell's Angel topic. I challenged him, asked lots of questions and expressed my opinion that I thought that the "charity work" was just a cover-up for some of the dark, sinister activities I've only heard about Hell's Angels. Of course, it's all hearsay of what I read or heard in the news over the years. I really didn't know much about them, but here I was expressing my uneducated opinion to a couple of "patched in" bikers.

Did I mention that riding a bike gave me some special level of confidence? Apparently, a special kind of stupid to some would argue. They seemed intriguing, and as the conversation continued, I asked what their patches meant. One of the guys said they belonged to a club called the Gatekeepers. He went on about how he had to get back to Ontario since a Prospect of his recently died. I was horrified; how sad is that. So, I continued to probe him with questions about this guy who died finding out worse yet - he was murdered. Yikes! At this point, I was ready to leave. I offered my condolences and wished them luck on their way back to Ontario. With the laundry complete, my husband and kids pulled up on the side of the road, and I quickly got in the vehicle. I was telling my family about my encounter with these two bikers and how they belonged to a club called the Gatekeepers. As we drove along, I Googled it to see if there was anything online that could tell me more about this motorcycle group/club. It turns out they are a self-proclaimed prospect club to the mothership of motorcycle clubs - the Hell's Angels. What?! And here I was calling the bluff on the do-good charity work of the Hell's Angels. A few days later we read about the death of this Prospect he was telling me about, their story checked out. I couldn't believe I was in a lengthy conversation with these two guys, and yet I thought nothing of it. Motorcycling brings all kinds of people together; it provides so much confidence and empowerment that yes even a 50-year-old mom can strike up a conversation with those real true-to-life bad-asses out there.

– Michelle Robart rides a M50 Suzuki Boulevard.

Meet Michelle Robart. She works as an administrator in the oil and gas sector in Alberta, Canada. Michelle joined the Canadian Forces at age 19 and served in the military for 20 years. She has been married for 28 years, and she tells us, they have two beautiful adult children. Her love of riding started at age 46 after taking a motorcycle safety riding course. And she has not looked back. Michelle says, "The people you meet and the places you visit while riding are hidden gems."

"DON'T TELL MY MOTHER"

We had an unspoken family rule. If one of my sisters or brothers lived beyond a 500-mile range, my parents did not want to know the particulars. Vague details were enough. My mother, after all, was a worrier.

When it came to my many missteps, of which there were too many to retell here, I was pretty grateful for this rule. So when I purchased my '07 Harley 883 XL Sportster last year, I was confident it fell under the don't ask, don't tell rule popularized under President Clinton.

Technically, I now live 300 or so miles from my mother. But since she moved from Florida to Massachusetts, I shoulder no responsibility. I live in New York and because she isn't prone to travel much, I feel fairly confident that my comings and goings are still invisible.

However, there is one more detail I should probably share with you. My mother just turned 90 in August. I just turned 59 and have not been on a motorcycle for at least 30 years.

Having just "weathered" the end of a relationship, and not gracefully so, it seemed as good a time as any for a diversion. I needed to regain some confidence. What better elixir can there be than riding a bike? More specifically, riding a Harley. So, I began my search and wondered how hard it would be to get my sea legs back.

Similar to how I handled most of my important life-changing decisions, I didn't consult anyone who was knowledgeable. I did, however, ask one of my younger friends who owns a sport bike shop via text if I could borrow a small bike for the road test. There was a pause in our text conversation.

"I am getting a Harley!" I texted with excitement. There was another pause.

He hemmed and hawed. He indeed had a bike that would work perfectly but told me it wasn't on the road or insured. It sounded fishy to me, but I gave him a pass.

He tried to talk me out of a Harley but I wasn't biting. He suggested I attend motorcycle school as the riding part of the licensing was waived. My nephew and brother-in-law suggested the same, telling me I would learn the same things.

"Sheesh!" I thought. "That stuff is for newbies."

I had been a confident urban rider who rode a vintage '65 BSA Lightning through the streets of Denver. My reliable commuter bike was a '69 Honda Dream, also known as a Honda Nightmare. But ours ran like a top as long as I pulled one plug, cleaned and lightly sanded it every 50 miles or so. Both bikes were beautiful and even Harley riders would give me a thumbs up as I limped around the city, mostly in clogs, shorts and sunglasses sans helmet. I was in my 30's and invincible.

But that was then. I got the hint from my conversations with my friends and family and reconsidered. I went to bike school and I did feel like a bit of a newbie. Not quite falling over, but not ready to hit the highway either. The instructors were sweet and there were some exceptional moments. One being when a very beginner student lost control of her bike, fixated on the instructor, and he literally had to leap out of the way. Knowing they were there to help increased my confidence, although my figure 8's were still suspect.

Forty years ago while in college, my first bike was a Kawasaki KZ 400. I would ride anytime - in the snow, with two friends on the back and one on the handlebars, plenty of insane moments. It was a great bike until my first intersection "incident." I knew with that scary slide that I was behaving too wildly and not mature enough to safely have a bike. I sold her and moved on. But since I am much older now, (ahem) my thinking was "if not now, when?"

I found my Harley on Facebook. Who doesn't these days? We texted back and forth, and the woman selling it seemed nice. I grabbed a friend, rented a truck and we drove deep into the hills of Pennsylvania. The bike started right up and looked pretty great. In my excitement, I didn't realize at the time that all that chrome should be shiny and not pitted, and the tires should not be so funky looking. They were throwing in a helmet and both she and her husband said it was a good bike. My friend, who knows less about bikes than I do, believed them too. It was a woman's bike, after all, and it's easy to trust women because we are women and we are powerful and honest! So, off we went without even test riding the bike because they firmly explained it wasn't current on tags or insurance. They did seem like nice people and the price was right so I didn't think it mattered.

On that cold, rainy April afternoon, I dropped my pal off and unloaded the bike. I threw on the previous owner's cigarette smoke filled helmet (how long does that scent last?), and wobbled on down my street. I felt unsteady, unsure, and scared. Finally, I felt old and thought "WTF did I do?" I somehow managed to ride the bike into my garage, eventually found neutral and shut her down. I was simultaneously frightened and thrilled.

Another friend, Ernie, had agreed to work on my bike. He owns a bike shop in Haynesville, New Jersey and is an award-winning, custom Harley builder who makes beautiful, creative, interesting bikes. I wanted some new doodads to freshen it up a bit. I had a few ideas in mind and trusted his creative instinct. I knew the two of us would come to a good place.

When he brought my refurbished bike back, it was a beautiful, updated, improved machine with a groovy Roland

Sands Air Cleaner, Vance and Hines short pipes, Metzler tires, all fluids replaced and tuned up. She looked amazing. I told Ernie that she looked sweet. He looked at me as if I just landed from Mars and said "It's a Harley. It is f**ing bad ass."

Now, I can't agree more. I have regained some confidence and skill on the bike and am riding the rubber off of the tires. While I am close to tucking her away for the winter, there are still some good days ahead. My mother still doesn't know.

– Mo Petkus is currently riding a 2007 Harley-Davidson 883 XL Sportster.

Meet Mo Petkus, *she is a Buddhist and the owner of Mo's Tonic, a small batch aromatherapy product company. She teaches high school and says, "I am still in love with my bike. I plan on riding until I forget how to find first gear." You can find out more about her tonic business at FB: Mo's Tonic or Website:* Barryvilleorganic.com

AM I TOO...

"My darling girl, when are you going to realize that being normal is not necessarily a virtue? It rather denotes a lack of courage."
- Aunt Frances, Practical Magic

When I got my motorcycle endorsement, I was lucky enough to be surrounded by women and men who also ride. Kathy and Bill, Cathy, Deb and my husband Dan, were all encouraging and helpful as I learned to ride my own motorcycle. I can't imagine the bravery it takes for a woman who has never ridden before to wake up one day and say, "I am going to ride my own motorcycle." Embracing the journey without support from family and friends. I think it is a real testament to those women and their rebel souls. May we all be like them when we grow up. – Sarah Andreas

A MIDLIFE CRISIS MADE BEAUTIFUL

"Omg! I cannot believe you got a motorcycle!"
"Did you just wake up today and decide to buy a one?"
"What are you thinking?"
"Are you going through a mid-life crisis?"
"You are crazy?"
"There are too many stupid people on the roads!"
"You are going to kill yourself."

All of the above are comments I heard from people when I bought my first ever motorcycle this past June. Yes, I had a mid-life crisis, and it was made beautiful.

On September 26th, I turned 50 years old. I'm a single mother with two daughters, two granddaughters, two female dogs and I work for a boss who is frequently compared to Miranda Priestly in the *Devil Wears Prada* by my coworkers. I've been married and divorced three times, and I have always been a people pleaser afraid to voice my own, true opinion until I bought my motorcycle.

I had only ridden a motorcycle once in my life. I was in high school and I don't think I even shifted the gears. I have been a passenger only once as well. Needless to say, I had no clue how to ride.

In 2010, I saw a lady on a Harley Sportster next to me at a light. I was headed to a local pub to watch a football game. She was going to the same place, and she ended up sitting next to me at the bar. We talked about her bike, and she made some recommendations should I ever decide to get one. After our exhilarating conversation, I decided I was going to be like her someday. Seven years later, that decision came to pass.

Over this past Memorial Day Weekend, I was with my youngest daughter in San Antonio, Texas, for a beach volleyball tournament. It was a Sunday and she didn't have any games so we decided to visit the Riverwalk. We walked into the Harley-Davidson shop to look around. A week later I was online checking to see what I would qualify for financially, just out of curiosity. I was immediately approved for more bike than I needed and the next day received a phone call from a local dealership offering me to come in for a fitting.

I was so excited and went to the dealership alone with no one but myself. I didn't call anyone to tell them what I was doing nor did I know anyone who rode. I arrived at the dealership and a few hours later was the proud owner of a 2017 Harley-Davidson Sportster 1200T SuperLow. The entire experience was absolutely liberating! I had just taken the biggest leap of faith I had ever taken in my life and knew my life was about to change forever...for the better.

A week later my bike was delivered to me and parked in my garage. I didn't even know how to turn the beast on. The following week I took the motorcycle safety course to learn how to ride. I didn't realize I would also be tested for an 'M' endorsement and on testing day, I failed the test. Devastated and defeated, I wondered if I had just made the biggest mistake of my life.

Fortunately, I had a motivated instructor who believed in me. He called my attention to an article online. The first sentence was congratulating me on failing my test and giving me advice on what to do next. After reading this article, I realized I knew enough and was capable enough to ride to a local parking lot and practice when no one was there. I was able to practice slow maneuvers, coming to a complete stop and shifting gears more smoothly. I had driven manual transmission cars for the majority of my life so shifting really wasn't the problem for me. It was maneuvering that beast of a machine slowly which challenged and defeated me during testing time. Plus, I was so tense that I looked like a tree trying to ride a broomstick.

Since the end of June, I have put almost 1200 miles on my seat riding locally and one round trip of 148 miles. I have never been happier in my life. I have met some amazing, like-minded people and my social life has exploded. My daughters are proud of me, my coworkers are impressed with me, and my self-esteem has never been higher. I am getting a toned and fit body from the strengthening that comes from mastering a near 700-pound beast at 60mph, or even two miles per hour for that matter. I am more aware of my world, noticing sights and smells I never would have in a cage.

Before I made the decision to pursue this newly discovered love and hobby, I was stressed out with no social life at all. I lived to work and worked to live. My social life consisted of me taking my youngest daughter to volleyball practices and attending her volleyball games. My oldest lives on her own and is attending nursing school, so she only calls or needs me occasionally. At night during the week, I would be in bed by nine pm. Not because of physical exhaustion but because of boredom or stress from the workday. The weekends I didn't have my daughter or volleyball, I would spend in front of the TV or on social media reading about everyone else's vacations and fun lives.

I was very much alone. That has all changed now and I am feeling better than I ever have in my life!

In November, I am taking my Motorcycle Safety Course again. This time I am confident I will pass with flying colors. Wish me luck!

– Lori Meredith is currently riding a 2017 Harley-Davidson Sportster 1200T Superlow.

Meet Lori Meredith. She is a 50-year-old single mother who works in mergers and acquisitions for a company that acquires veterinary practices and pet resorts. She has a Bachelor's of Science Degree and has worked in the corporate world since graduating from college in 2002. She has never had a hobby she's loved as much as riding her motorcycle.

RIDING HAS NO AGE LIMIT!

Having always loved motorcycles since I was a teenager, or maybe younger. My dad gave me a rided on the gas tank as a small child. When I was a Junior in high school, I signed up for a motorcycle course offered. I had heard my older sister, who was a Senior, said she signed up for the course too. Oh boy, I could see it now, being teased so badly if I made a mistake, as teenage angst set in, so I withdrew from the class. My boyfriend, who became my husband, got a motorcycle when he was 19 of which I loved riding on the back of and holding him tight! After we got married, started a family young and had two sons, it was time for the motorcycle to go, but not until after my husband had a few slides and a car hitting him from behind.

When my oldest son worked at AutoZone as a teenager, he convinced me to buy a Pocket Rocket the store just got in, for he and his brothers to ride. I figured that a 25cc bike like that would be easy to ride, fun for all. My husband was against it from the beginning and a little angry with me that I bought it, so he stated matter of factly that no one was going to ride it until I purchased a helmet. I purchased a helmet, and we got set to ride with many of the kids, their dad's looking on at the new toy we purchased. I wanted to be the 1st rider since I had purchased it, so I donned the helmet, set forth on the end of the driveway with all my sons, their dad, neighborhood boys and their fathers witnessing my first ride. It seemed easy enough to me as no shifting of gears, and I wondered...how hard can it be? I take off and realize it is not as easy as I had thought. I saw my trajectory heading towards the neighbor's driveway, and I quickly assess that jumping into the neighbors' grass was better than hitting the pavement of the driveway, so I did just that. I stood up, very embarrassed, stated I was okay, while silently my hip and my arm were throbbing with pain but probably more of my pride hurt than anything else.

I felt a little intimidated at that point about riding. Over the years of marriage, I had asked my husband if he would get another motorcycle since he knew how much I have loved riding on them. His memories of three small accidents always prevented him from pulling that trigger until we decided to buy new bicycles in the summer of 2015. We had a blast riding our bicycles and I asked him upon returning home after our long rides, "Hey, let's go look at motorcycles," to which he replied "No," on two occasions. The third time I asked, he said YES! *Who knew, right?* Even though he was experienced at riding, he took the riding course the following weekend. We ended up purchasing a '16 HD Road Glide Ultra at HD in Kansas City shortly after. This was our first Harley Davidson experience, which was absolutely awesome! While at the dealership, I spied the 2016 Softail Deluxe in Frosted Teal/Crushed Ice Pearl. This became my dream bike as I fell in love with the styling, colors and decided that was to be my goal in 2016 since it was my 50th Birthday year!

I waited until spring of '16, just a few months after turning 50, to get my 1st bike! It was a Yamaha V-Star 650 Classic. I had not taken the riding course yet, but I felt this was a good fit for me. My husband took me to a nearby parking lot, taught me the basics of which he told me he was highly impressed how quickly I picked it all up, and by day two, I was shifting into 2nd, 3rd gears. He thought I was moving too quickly through it all, but he realized I was a very good student! I was so excited about it, and I knew this was my time! I enjoyed riding around through the city with my husband as my riding buddy, but I kept my "dream bike" close in proximity as I felt I was outgrowing the V-Star quicker than I had anticipated. In summer of that year, we happened to be in Kansas City for a concert, and stopped by the dealership so I could "test ride" a few bikes and what do 'ya know...I bought my dream bike! I had her delivered the next day with my family all present with the unveiling out of the trailer. This was HUGE to me!

My youngest son, who was studying to be an engineer, had a scary look on his face when they took my new Harley out of the trailer. I asked him what was the matter? I later found out he was thinking of all the power of this bike vs. my V-Star which worried him. My youngest son even bought his motorcycle and his older brother rode with us often before I sold my V-Star. I love riding with my boys, and my husband is my favorite riding buddy...but I do like to get out on my own to stretch my wings and the solitude can be cathartic! I have adventures planned for my future of heading to Sturgis someday, riding through New Mexico, Arizona and lower Utah to Forrest Gump Point, and maybe an awesome girls trip might be fun too. With having an autoimmune disease, I do find it takes me a bit longer to recuperate, and pain in my hands can make it challenging, but I still get out there and do it because I DON'T RIDE A BIKE TO ADD DAYS TO MY LIFE. I RIDE TO GIVE LIFE TO MY DAYS!
– Danielle L, Wood rides a 2016 Harley Davidson Softail Deluxe.

Meet Danielle Wood from Kansas. She is a Real Estate Agent. Danielle has been married for 32 years to her high school sweetheart. They have four awesome sons. And she has four grandchildren!

LIFE AFTER 40

I had always ridden on the back of the motorcycle with boyfriends when I was younger. I never thought I could learn to ride on my own and never had anyone to encourage me, but then I turned 40 and decided I was tired of not living and being with someone that was always angry. So I got my first tattoo and a divorce, then a guy that rode and life started changing but then I got bored when he was gone with his friends riding, and I was stuck at home. So I asked him to teach me, he encouraged me to take the motorcycle safety course if I wanted to learn and then I got my first bike, a Honda Shadow 600. I love this little girl, but she scared me also. Every time I took her out my legs would shake so badly, and I stalled her out at lights, and on hills. I made so many stupid mistakes because I was so scared. It's a wonder I am still alive. I dropped her in parking lots having to replace her mirrors several times, and I even broke my arm once, that was a lesson learned, but I persevered never giving up my dream. Then I joined my first women's riding group, Women on Wheels in Augusta, Georgia. These women gave me the courage to keep riding and my sense of freedom. I was no longer that scared woman that never ventured out; I moved away from everyone I knew and made new friends and new adventures but was still not that fearless person I wanted to be. I made several trips from Marietta to Augusta on my bike by myself (it was about a 167-mile trip one way) took way longer than the 2 ½ hours that it would take in the car.

I then got the courage to take a job in Ontario, New York, I sold my bike thinking I won't have a place to store it and I don't know a soul in NY. Once I got to NY I started to feel sad that I sold my bike and started looking for a new one, I wound up buying a used Kawasaki Vulcan and met an older lady that became my best friend that had rode when she was younger, and she was seriously thinking about riding again. I also found out my neighbor and my friend wanted to learn to ride, so I encouraged both of these new NY friends to ride and with these new friends came more brave and strong women, the more of them that I met, the stronger I became. I dared to take on different positions with my job in different places in NY and meet more people. I have decided my moving days are over and found an awesome area to stay in and have recently joined the Stilettos on Steel female riders group. They are a great bunch of women that help one another and are down to earth. My ride these days is a 2010 Harley Davidson Dyna Wide Glide that I bought myself for my 50th birthday. My dream is to ride across the country from New York to California and beyond one day and have that most awesome adventure for myself.

So yes there is life after 40 or 50, no matter where or when you start, life changes when you learn to ride on your own. You become stronger and braver and feel that you can take on the world.

– Deborah Mitchum, 2010 Harley Davidson Dyna Wide Glide.

Meet Deborah Mitchum. *She is a Consumer Safety Inspector with the United States Department of Agriculture in Endicott, NY.*

#RIDINGWITHSTEPHEN

My riding story started 12 years ago when my husband decided to quit drag-racing. He not only quit, but he sold his race car, and after 25 years without a motorcycle, he came home with a bike. We hadn't spent much time together after our daughter left home, as I threw myself into four years of college and earned my BA; while Stephen ran his repair business, played in a band, and drag-raced. But, suddenly after years of these solo pursuits, we were about to reconnect through motorcycling together.

That first year I tried to be a passenger, but as we spent more and more of our free time on the road, I was finding it hard. Before long Stephen was prodding me, and encouraging me, to get my license so I could have my own bike. Now I didn't need much prompting since--as a tomboy--I had loved my bicycle and was glued to it. I was anticipating that a motorcycle of my own could bring back those wonderful carefree days. And so, that winter--when I sat on a Honda Rebel during a Winter Bike Show and discovered that at 5' 2" I could reach the ground--I was all in!!

Just weeks later my husband surprised me with a Rebel of my own! Waiting for spring was hard but finally "warm-enough" weather came. I was lucky that my husband's business was next to a car lot. On Sundays, they'd move a few cars so I could practice riding in the lot. And...this is where I had the first of those "learning-to-ride" moments that we all fear - I dropped it! It was my second time riding, and I stalled the bike and fell over. Hard. Hit-my-helmet-on-the-pavement-<u>hard</u>. Why-you'll-never-see-me-without-a-helmet--<u>hard</u>. I'd insisted on practicing alone due to being self-conscious, so I had to manage the bike back onto its wheels myself. By pure adrenaline I got it standing. I was a little shook up, a little bruised, but determined-

27

-in that "get back on the horse" sort of way--and I prevailed. Ultimately, I clocked over 30 miles in that parking lot (that's when I started keeping track of my miles). Finally, the weekend of my Rider Safety course arrived--by the way, one of the best things I did for myself! The instructors were amazing and inspired confidence. By the end of the weekend, I'd earned my endorsement. Stephen was so proud of me, but I was nervous about actual road riding, considering that all my riding so far had been in parking lots! So, we rode together right from the start.

I rode 300 miles on the Rebel my first month, but it was just a little too "up-straight" for me. Then, I had the chance to try a Yamaha Virago 250. With its forward controls, pullback bars, and a lower seat, the 300-pound bike was perfect and not physically overwhelming for someone who'd just turned 53. I was in love. We were made for each other.

Our first season riding together, Stephen set a safety standard for me that I follow to this day--all the gear, all the time! (my first fall drove home the need for a helmet). After all, he not only drag-raced cars but flew airplanes, holds aircraft mechanic's licenses and does welding...all of which require safety gear. So, we "dress for the slide, not the ride!" And maybe it was because record-keeping was central to both flying and drag-racing, that he liked the idea of keeping track of our miles together on our own "riding calendar." We love posting our miles at the end of a great ride.

One of the biggest ways Stephen supports my riding is that he watches my back. I ride in front, toward the road's edge and he rides behind me--toward the center. I also ride lead because I'm a natural navigator, but in deference to my novice status, I stay near the side of the road. Additionally, he can always see what I'm doing (or doing wrong...lol) and I am circumstantially always checking my mirrors, more so than I might if he weren't behind me.

We ride every chance we get. Here in Vermont, we are on the road as soon as it's 50 degrees--no matter what month it is. We have ridden during every calendar month except February. We even rode Christmas Eve in 2015! I wear an LL Bean down ski-coat and snow pants when we ride in the "winter" months. What I'm saying is--riding is our shared passion!

Riding has become central to our marriage since Stephen's retirement. We've motorcycled all around New England. (He proudly jokes that I know every road for 200 miles). We've traveled to both the mountains and the ocean, but mostly we do day-trips. Don't be fooled by that, though; one of our favorites is a 200-mile round-trip for chicken-n-biscuits at the Halfway House Restaurant. A ride we call the "winner-winner-chicken-dinner-run." With my smartphone in hand, I document all of our riding adventures; Facebook hashtagged #RidingWithStephen.

For more than half of my ten years riding, I've had serious health problems from three separate Lyme disease infections. Although this has slowed me down, I have not been counted out yet; I still managed to ride 6,700 miles this year (2017). Whenever I feel strong enough, I am on my bike. And because of the incredible emotional (and mechanical) support of my husband, this 63-year-old woman has 83,404 miles of seat-time in just ten years. Back in 2007, when I got my endorsement, my goal was to ride 100,000 miles. And although at my age I know it's not a given, with only 17,000 miles to go, I think I'll reach that goal—it's within sight. After all, I'm riding with the support of my best friend; I'm #RidingWithStephen
– Debra Deming Walsh, Yamaha Virago 250

Meet Debra Deming Walsh. She claims to be a 63-year-old Vermont hippie. On December 6th she and her husband celebrated their 37th anniversary. Professionally, she is semi-retired. She was self-employed as a commercial seamstress, specializing in slipcovers and window treatments for 38 years. Her husband is also retired from owning an auto repair business. They have been empty-nesters for 18 years. Debra says that "Currently, we find nothing more thrilling than waking up 'retire' on a beautiful day, and having nothing more pressing than spending our entire day riding our bikes."

RIDING OUTSIDE OF THE BOX.

In 2004 I started a new chapter in my life. Something I had wanted to do since I was a young girl – Ride a Motorcycle. Believe it or not, I was at work and just sitting there daydreaming the thoughts – in a few months my son will graduate from high school. I no longer will be volunteering at his school, my husband is always away working on a boat so what is a girl to do? I handled my empty nest differently than most. I thought, "hmm, time to do what I've wanted to do for the past 30 years – get a motorcycle and learn to ride." So I searched for an MSF course, signed up and did it all within a week. That included the course, purchase a motorcycle and got my endorsement. Boom it was done. My son even went with me to purchase my first motorcycle, and he thought and said: "Mom, you are crazy." I told him, "Nope, I've been waiting way too long, and now it is time." That was now over 14 years ago. My life has changed forever. In a nutshell, I've made lifelong friends I've met on the road from the 10th anniversary 911 event in NY City to my US 4 Corners Ride in 2016. Lifelong friends through social media on motorcycle pages who I later met in person and continue to be friends with. I joined the best and oldest women's motorcycling club in the US/Canada – the Motor Maids and they, alone, have been empowering.

As a new rider in 2004, I had no idea what I just got myself into. In fact, the person who sold me my first motorcycle warned my husband that I'd never get off. I'd say he was pretty darn close. It's not always been an easy ride. I learned to educate myself to become a better rider, and to this day I'm still learning. I've battled many health issues that I thought might stop my dream of riding but I never gave up. There was one time after a serious illness and surgery I looked at my bike in my garage differently but with the willpower and the help of some awesome friends I got back on and regained my strength to do a longtime goal of mine. Finally – the US 4 Corners Ride. It was an emotional moment reaching the final 4th corner in San Ysidro, California. The feeling was overwhelming. I actually have a Sticky Note on my desk at home that says "Where to Next?" So now that I've ridden in 49 of the 50 states, I'll be focusing on Alaska in 2019 along with a coast to coast ride. I kind of did my goals in baby steps.

2006 – Solo ride around the State of Texas
2007 – Solo ride out of the state to New Mexico/Colorado
2011 – Border to Border ride from Mexico to Canada
2015 – Solo ride from Moncton, British Columbia, Canada to home
2016 – US 4 Corners Ride (Florida, Maine, Washington, and California)
2004-2017 – Total of 49 US states including Mexico and Canada
Approximately a total of 232,000+ miles and still counting!

I taught myself to go outside my box, my street, my neighborhood, my area, my state and my country. You just never know what and who you'll find. In Newburgh, NY, amongst 3,000 motorcycle riders who came together for a ride to honor those lost on 911, a firefighter Captain from Anaheim, CA. We have continued our friendship for over six years. He, in turn, met a friend of mine several years later in the desert in NV. I've made great friends all over the US, Canada, Australia, and Ireland. All because of getting out and riding my motorcycle. In 2016 on my US 4 Corners Ride I met an inspirational woman who too was riding on her US 4 Corners Ride at the ME welcome center. We've shared stories and support each other like we've been friends for life.

Just get out and ride. Take a chance and ride outside the box. You'll never know what or who you'll find.
– Laura Wright Goldenschue, 2014 Harley-Davidson CVO Deluxe and a 1999 BMW R1200C

Meet Laura Wright Goldenschue, she says she is a Texas girl and has been riding for 14 years. Laura is a retired bookkeeper and spends most of her time riding her motorcycle or planning her next ride. In '09 she helped start the Women's Riding and Mentoring Group at a local Harley-Davidson dealership to mentor new women riders until '12 when they moved it to The Women Who Love to Ride Meet-Up. In '09 she joined the Motor Maids and later became the District Director for the Texas chapter for five years. Laura says, "I continue to mentor new riders and believe we mentor every day whether we know it or not."

DREAMS DO COME TRUE!

My obsession with motorcycles began in my teens. I had my permit in my 20s and rode a friend's bike. Then marriage and kids became the priority. I finally followed through in my 50s! I hit my most recent goal of 1000 miles in my first three months of riding. One of my first goals, when I bought my motorcycle, was just to be able to ride the five miles to work. I would ride one and a half miles down the road to a parking lot, practice turns and come home. I dumped it twice and hurt my knee and ankle. A little setback, but I got back on and kept going. I learned from my mistakes, and now I am so proud and happy to say that I have successfully put over 1000 miles on my bike! Something I have always desired to do, not realizing how happy it would make me. My bigger goal is to eat fish tacos in Baja while I tour the peninsula on my motorcycle. Dreams do come true!

– Seton Tomford rides a 2008 Suzuki GZ250.

Meet Seton Tomford. She is from New York. She is the fifth of seven sisters. She works in a small credit union in her hometown in New York.

COOL GRANDMAS

"You'll learn, as you get older that rules are made to be broken. Be bold enough to live life on your terms, and never, ever apologize for it. Go against the grain, refuse to conform, take the road less traveled instead of the well-beaten path. Laugh in the face of adversity, and leap before you look. Dance as though EVERYBODY is watching. March to the beat of your own drummer. And stubbornly refuse to fit in." — Mandy Hale, The Single Woman: Life, Love, and a Dash of Sass

NO PERMISSION NEEDED!

The first time I got on a bike I was 16, I dated a guy who rode, I knew at that moment that someday I would ride my own. I always wanted to ride but, as it does, life got in the way. I had an (ex) husband who was not supportive. Then I became a single mom and neither the money or the time were there. At 49 years old, when my daughter was out on her own and I had a supportive husband who encouraged me, I did it! I bought a bike, took the class and got endorsed.

Now at 51, it's my second riding season and I ride as much as I possibly can. Family members don't agree. My daughter is strongly against it, but the first time I was on my bike something inside of me came alive. I felt the most excitement and freedom I had never known. Every time I'm on my Skittles (that's what I call my bike) and she comes to life, I hear the rumble of my pipes and hit the road everything else just disappears. From that moment on it's just me, my bike, the open road and a sense of complete freedom that I have never felt before. Next year I'm hoping to take an out of state trip. My advice to you is, if you have the urge to ride, do it now. You

won't regret it. My only regret is that I waited so long.
– Lori Himmelstein currently rides a 2008 Harley Davidson
Sportster 1200 named Skittles

Meet Lori Himmelstein, she is 51 years old and lives in Menomonee Falls, Wisconsin. She has been working for the same company for 21 years and now is in upper management. Lori tells us she is married to a very supportive man who always encourages her to go for what she believes in. She has a 28-year-old daughter and a 2-year-old granddaughter who have stolen her heart. She is also a dog-mom to an 11-year-old dog. Besides riding, some of her hobbies include hiking, camping, really anything that can be done outside and spending as much time as possible with her family!

NINJA NANA LEARNS TO RIDE

Approximately 25 years ago I successfully completed the written test for my learner motorbike license. My ex-husband rode bikes, but he did not have a license and was not very encouraging when it came to me learning to ride. I decided to sign up for a riding course way back then, but only did a few hours and was so embarrassed because I had no idea how to ride. I didn't go back again. Eventually, I just forgot about getting a motorbike license altogether.

Fast-forward approximately 23 years. Many things had happened, including divorce and a new marriage. One day while I was fueling up my car, I noticed a nice looking white motorbike at the next petrol pump. As I walked past the bike admiring it, a young woman walked past me and proceeded to get on the bike and rode off. I was so impressed that not only was she a young woman, but she was tiny as well. When I arrived home, I told my husband and teenage son about the young woman who rode off on the white bike. It rekindled the interest of learning to ride again. I thought if she can do it, then so can I.

Our teenage son owns an XR250, and I started to learn on this. Because we live in a rural area, I was able to take his bike out and practice on our two acres as well as take the bike out the back of our block. I found the kickstart hard to handle and had massive bruises on the back of my leg. His bike is heavy and I dropped it a few times, usually while attempting to stop. After a few weeks, I told hubby I needed a bike with an electric start. I also borrowed a helmet from one of our daughters. Her husband tried teaching her to ride on dirt tracks, but she decided at this time it's not for her.

My husband looked for a bike he thought suitable for me. He enjoys riding around sightseeing as well as trail riding. I ended up with a KLX250. I rode around our two acres weaving around trees and gardens. We started riding on the dirt roads so I could get the feel of the bike. I dropped my bike a couple of times but got back up and continued riding. Eventually, as I became more confident, we started riding on the bitumen. At first it was just our local area. But gradually as I gained more confidence, we started riding into other small local rural villages. Then I decided I needed town riding, so hubby would load his DRZ400 and my KLX250 onto the trailer and we would go into town and ride the bikes in traffic and roundabouts and stoplights.

I was booked to go for my motorbike license on 7th February 2017, but just 10 days before, while practicing turning and weaving in the council carpark, I dropped the bike and smashed a bone in my foot. Two months later I was back on the bike. I bought my own white full-face helmet, gloves and riding boots and a second-hand riding jacket...I was getting serious at that point.

More riding, more towing the bikes so we could ride around the suburbs as I wanted/needed experience riding in traffic under different conditions.

I booked myself in for the riding test once again. This time I had to cancel to attend the funeral of one of my brothers. He was flying a small plane which crashed. I found out he also had a love for motorbikes, especially his Harley.

I re-booked a third time, this time more determined than ever to actually take the test and to pass. This time I knew my brother was going to be with me in spirit.

15 months after initially throwing a leg over my son's bike, on 12th August 2017 at the tender age of 56 just a few weeks shy of my 57th birthday, I participated in the 7.5-hour riding test. There were four young male learner riders in the course

with me. We were all successful. It was a long, hot day, but I am so proud of myself for finding the confidence to keep trying and keep going.

I must also acknowledge my very patient husband who rode with me every weekend loading the bikes on and off the trailer and encouraging me all the way.

My dream now is to buy a white bike, possibly a Kawasaki Ninja and a white jacket, possibly leather. My grandkids sometimes call me "Ninja Nana" because I have a black belt in TaeKwonDo, so a Ninja bike would be fitting I reckon. How cool would it be to have Ninja Nana painted on my bike and helmet?

In November Tracey updated her bike. She said, I threw my leg over a brand new z300 as well as a bigger bike and decided to buy a white z300. I am now the proud owner of my "little green machine" and my soon to be "naked ninja." After having a learner's permit for a bike for 25 years and finally getting my open RE license 3 months ago, I proudly own 2 bikes.

Why did I wait so long? ☐
– Tracey Byrne is currently riding a z300.

Meet Tracey Byrne, she is a 57-year-old mother of 6 and has 7 grandchildren so far. She lives in a small rural community in Queensland, Australia, where she works as a Teacher's Aide in their tiny local school of 12 children. Many years ago, she started training with a TaeKwonDo club and after a few years, she earned her 1st-degree Blackbelt. She hopes that by writing her story people can see they can do anything they want whether they are male or female, young or old. She says, "If you set your mind to it, you can do anything."

ENCHANTED FOREST FLOOR OF SHROOMDOM!

I began riding a street bike first, about age 35 because I refused to be a hugger! I had been riding horses since I was 17 so throwing a leg over was easy, getting used to the dangers of the road meant Motorcycle Safety and Gear!

My real adventures on a bike began when I sold my first street bike and took a guy with me for a ten-hour ride to purchase a new street bike. We began a relationship a few years later which has led to marriage. My husband always wished for someone to ride with well he got more than he wished for, he got my two granddaughters and me.

One day I took off on Tony's son's Honda 70 across the wildflower field behind his house came back and said, "Let's go, I have got to have a dirtbike." At the age of 44, I began riding Dirt, or eating it for a while. I ride a Honda 150 R; I also won a SWAG of the month from Dirt Rider for this bike. We have an MX track and trails on our 160-acre Mushroom farm that runs through the Enchanted Forest floor of Shroomdom! I had a time adjusting to this bike as street riding does not cross over.

So many longest rides. First was six-hours on the road through Baton Rouge, Louisiana, and back...wow, I made it and I didn't get hit. Next, in the rain over a swing bridge...thank God I didn't go down, my arms, neck and shoulders were tight for days, yes, I hung on for dear life! Next came the dirt on the track up over the berm...missed my turn on the Apex. I flew through over the top into the pine trees, I landed it on the back wheel and kept going!

By now my granddaughters were old enough to start riding, so I started them on 50PW Yamaha's as they grew I moved them to 110 electric Starts Yamaha BLUE! Next, I said, "Hey at age 51 let's take a class on trails, bikes, and HOP ROCKS!" What's a husband to say to the woman who's full of

Moxie and will do it without him? Yep, let's go.

I have now purchased and ride a Sherco trials bike have taken a class with six-time National Champion Ryan Young. Wish I could say I play with GRAVITY - more like it plays with me - I'm hanging tough. This is where my true longest ride has been, following Ryan, terrified yes, but again, up the Powerlines of Saddleback Riding Club in Kentucky taking a hard left into the wooded trails with a huge drop-off and up a waterfall! I literally hung on, prayed, and cried on this one!

I hope my granddaughters gain all that I have from being a rider and add to the list, as the world is forever wide open for them! Never follow a man, stand beside him, and if need be, stand alone. Basic mechanics, how to just twist it and keep it on at least one wheel, back is always a good choice. Heck with (shoes) BOOTS, Helmets, Roost Guard, Silks and an Awesome Helmet GEAR, YEAH…LOTS OF GEAR!

You don't have to be a Babe, you can be a woman who can ride like the wind and darn well mean it…and do it alone cause you just LOVE the sheer joy of throwing your leg over your Steel Horse revving the engine and just twisting that throttle! Most of all that when you're truly scared and you want to do it, PRAY! It's never failed me ever not once!

– Leilani Rosenbaum (Riding and Loving it, cause life is about the RIDE! Riding with those you LOVE make it Extra Sweet!)

Meet Leilani Rosenbaum from Mississippi. She was born on Oahu, Hawaii and she says she was a Navy Brat! She is the mother of four children, and the grandmother of two girls. She rides dirt with them. Leilani says that her husband is an awesome man who has encouraged her in so many ways. He even helped her to become a certified Mississippi Volunteer Fire Fighter and First Responder. She is a Certified

Diver, Nitrox and Advance. They learned to snow ski in their late 40's. Leilani is also proud that she is a certified Heavy Equipment operator. She says, "Tony made my life time dream come true, I'm a FARMER!" They built their farm together in Mississippi. They do field to forest farm, harvest wild edibles from the forest floor, cultivate gourmet mushrooms and keep bees in AZ hives from Slovenia. They practice conservation stewardship at all times wherever they are. She says that their rest and relaxation is Riding Dirt and at times when she is eating it!
Visitmississippi.org or email her Shroomdom38@outlook.com

NEW HIGHWAYS AND HORIZONS

I grew up in the country, lots of space for roaming and riding. My dad kept us kids on dirt bikes and scooters to ride and play on. With five kids in the family and numerous cousins around, there was always someone to ride with.

I can vividly remember seeing my first chopper. I wasn't 16 yet, was in the backseat of my parent's car and a long dark haired guy on a red chopper passed us on the highway...I can still see him, and his bike, like it was yesterday.

I graduated from high school in 1981 and in late 1982 met my soon to be husband. He was fine and rode a 1947 Harley Davidson Knucklehead that he had rebuilt, at the time I wouldn't have known anything about a Knucklehead at all, but I was schooled by one of the best! It was a sharp bike, and he swept me off of my feet. We rode that Knucklehead for years but as we got older (he was 16 years older than I), riding a hardtail on these Oklahoma roads took a toll on our backs and rear ends. We upgraded to a '83 Shovelhead and then in 2007 purchased a brand new 2007 Heritage Softail Classic. It was a dream to ride, we'd go on long weekend trips with friends and long day rides exploring our area.

Suddenly on August 9, 2010, I lost my husband of 27 plus years. I was devastated, but the evening after his funeral a few friends and I went for about a 30-mile ride. I had ridden other bikes we'd had but never the Heritage on my own. I was so unsure of myself and upset with the entire situation. I had a large group of close friends and family at the house, and I promptly dropped the bike before we ever got out of the back yard. I was in the grass, and nothing was hurt except my pride. There were no other mishaps, but I left the bike parked until spring of 2011, I didn't go out on my own for some time.

I finally decided I could do it, I rode about 40 miles and took a route where I knew plenty of people in case I had problems. I got home, pulled into the garage and got off the bike so proud of myself but forgot to put the kickstand down and it laid down on the left crash bar! I was able to right it on my own, and I posted about my adventure that night on Facebook. One has to be able to laugh at herself, several of my friends congratulated me on my solo ride then gave me a hard time about forgetting the kickstand but at the same time admitted that they had done the same thing. It was a well-learned lesson that hasn't been repeated.

I had a good friend from Texas call, he asked me to meet him and his wife in Conway, Arkansas, and we'd ride the Pig Trail over a long weekend. It was my first LONG solo trip and my first trip across state lines! I was nervous and excited! I mapped out my route and knew where I was going to meet them and made it without getting lost once! It was a great success! We spent four days riding around Arkansas and did great. I was ready for anything!

In 2014 a friend who had grown up next door to Dot Robinson had sent me an article and said to check out the

Motor Maids. I called the Oklahoma Motor Maid district director and joined January of '14. It was the best phone call I have ever made! The Motor Maids and the ladies I've met have been life savers! I'm now the Oklahoma district director and enjoy every minute of it! I enjoy spreading the word about Motor Maids and meeting women riders and helping them feel comfortable in the saddle (if they are less than comfortable).

I have since been to the 2016 Motor Maid convention in Santa Fe New Mexico, paraded through Santa Fe with a large group of female riders from all across the US and Canada. While riding the area around Santa Fe, we went to Madrid and met about 15-20 Swedes on Harleys who had flown to Chicago, rented bikes and were riding across the US. We had a lovely visit with them. We rode to the top of Sandia Crest overlooking Albuquerque to enjoy the view. On the way home from Santa Fe, between Raton, NM and Trinidad, CO we got caught in a hail storm in the mountains!

Us Oklahoma Motor Maids and some from other states have presented the colors at the OKC Mile flat track races in Oklahoma City the last two years, something we are very proud of and honored to do.

I have ridden through Arkansas three times since that first trip; one trip was to the Dot Robinson field meet at Petit Jean, Arkansas. I've ridden parts of Texas, Louisiana, Tennessee, Colorado and all over our great state of Oklahoma!

It's a passion I'm so glad to have in my life. I can relax and recoup out on the road, I enjoy the sights and smells that you don't get in a vehicle. I enjoy photography and taking pics of my friends, their bikes, me and my bike.

— Barbara Payne Bennett rides a 2007 black Harley Davidson Heritage Softail Classic with just over 60,000 miles on it.

Meet Barbara Payne Bennett; she is from Oklahoma. Barbara is an Emergency Communication Professional (911 Operator/Emergency Services Dispatcher). She was the first 911 operator hired at Enid Police Department in 1990 and worked there until 2003. She worked for a few months at Garfield County Sheriff's Office and then started working at Stillwater Oklahoma Police Department in 2006 and is still dispatching for emergency services. She grew up out in the country, went to a very small school (32 in her graduating class of 1981). Barbara has grandkids, three girls, and a boy, and she hopes to instill the riding fever in them all! The two closest to her enjoy riding, and her son now has the Knucklehead and Shovelhead and is passing on the love and knowledge of bikes to his kids.

GOLDEN HEARTS

'It is the rider's willingness to share, help each other, support their communities that show the golden hearts under the black leather.'
— Sarah Andreas

"I find the members of my tribe, riding my Iron Horse."
- Sherry Burdick

As I started to get into motorcycling, I could have stopped riding after I dropped my bike on a ride with about twelve other women. But I didn't. We were coming up a hill that had a stop sign and about two feet of flat at the top. I had a problem with that same hill when I first learned to ride and when the group stopped, I made sure that I was close to the front of the group so I could stop on the flat. I had put my foot down to balance the bike, and there was no ground under my foot. The bike and I went over on the right side. I was very lucky that there was enough ground under the bike that it did not roll over on me and down the right embankment. The ladies behind me parked their bikes and helped me pick mine up. Then we rode to a straightaway, and Vicki the ride leader pulled over and everyone checked on me. I told Vicki, we needed to keep going. If we would have stopped then, I knew I would start crying and would not finish the ride. We kept going and when we got to our destination several other women shared their "me too" stories with me. It helped me feel better to know I wasn't alone. I never will forget their kindness and willingness to share. That is what makes the women who ride so special to me. They are a big part of why I didn't give up. – Sarah Andreas

ROAD QUEEN

I began riding as a fluke back in the 1970's. My dad had a 1968 Norton P11 750. Right-hand shift, kick-start. Hard to start as a matter of fact. One day he was working in the garage, and I said: "Hey Dad when you 'gonna sell me your bike?" I was told if I could start it in one kick he would sell it to me, so all 100 pounds of me got on that bike and BAM it started in ONE kick!

True to his word he sold it to me for 25 bucks a month. Boy was my mom mad when she got home! But the kicker of this story (no pun intended) was that it would be a long time before I could kick-start that bike again.

Since I was a teenager at the time, I could not afford a car and a bike so I only had the bike. I had to get to work to pay for my new toy, so I would go in the house and wake up my Dad and he would come outside, kick the bike over and go back to bed. I would ride to work and when the day was over the guys in the back would push me down the road so I could pop it into 2nd gear and go home. This went on for a couple of months until I learned to get my butt into it and start it on my own. At that point I was free to go anywhere. I could start it on my own. I remember this all like it was yesterday. I also remember that I never did pay off that motorcycle. Typical teenager I guess.

My current ride is a 2013 Harley Davidson Road Glide Ultra I bought new and has over 100k on it. I ride almost every day. I live, breathe, dream, dress and ride Harley Davidson. Motorcycles have definitely made me who I am today. I own the trademark "Road Queen" and run an organization called Road Queen USA that promotes women and motorcycling and riding for a cause. I have well over 500,000 miles under my belt. I have ridden to every state in the continental U.S. solo, mostly on back roads. It is all chronicled in pictures. I have been on *Born to Ride* TV with Jean Davidson, granddaughter of one of the founders of Harley Davidson, riding on the back of my motorcycle!

– Linda Dalton rides a 2013 Harley-Davidson Road Glide Ultra.

Meet Linda Dalton. She is the original Road Queen. She is from Lecanto, Florida, and has started an organization that does charitable work while riding their motorcycles. You can find more information at www.roadqueenusa.org

RIDING WITH A PASSION AND PURPOSE.

Beginning with my 1200 custom Sporty, aka Harley, I became familiar with the local back roads quickly. Finding my renewed passion for two wheels, I first reached out to friends to ride with on a local female bikers website. Where I met my long distance riding wind sister, Jaxx. We are two recently single women who had a passion for riding, and all the time to do it, so we started making plans.

Regular day trips turned into weekend trips turned into week trips and eventually up to month trips for me. The wind embraced me, and I reached into the wind and took flight. From popular local rides such as Harmony Grove, Elfin Forrest, Palomar Mountain, Mesa Grande Loop, Borrego, Julian, Hwy 101, Hwy 79, Historical Hwy 80 and beach coastal runs are just to name a few. The scenery was magnetic and left me wanting more. And although San Diego has much to offer, my curiosity lead me to branch out. Jaxx and I began making plans. Coming up, Babes Ride Out, aka BRO.

Then life threw a curve ball while visiting my son, his new bride, and an old high school friend up in Oregon. I was experiencing stiffness and pain in my right leg while having a lunch turn into dinner with an old high school friend. Chalking it up to age, sitting in one place too long, I made light of it and commented how my "body needs to warm up after sitting for a while these days before moving," and shrugged it off. Later that night I woke up about 2 am in pain and with no ability to put weight on my leg, and I had discovered that my right leg had no definition of knee or ankle. It looked like a log.

Calling the emergency room back home in San Diego I was urged to get back asap. Returning on an emergency medical flight from Oregon back to California, I was taken straight to the emergency room from the airport where I was diagnosed with Deep Vein Thrombosis (DVT) and was admitted. It was unexpected that my admission into the hospital would lead to surgery with a three-month stay for recovery and physical therapy rehabilitation. It was also during my stay in the hospital that I developed 97% drop foot and would need to add that to my PT schedule.

With intense treatment, three months later, and proving to the medical staff that I had built up my walking endurance and that I was stable with my walker, I was released with 24-hour care and medical staff scheduled to come to my home for six weeks.

Determined to walk and ride again I became intense and focused on my fight back. And I did it! My goal to make it to BRO with wind sister Jaxx was accomplished, and the wheels have been rolling ever since.

I am a woman in the wind and will be seen on my Road King with a smile, sharing a wave, nod, salute, and sharing riding experiences with kids and their parents who admire my bike.

I keep bandanas, scarfs, and hair ties on my bike to hand them out to kids and encourage safe and fun riding. After sharing an adventure or two I give a gift to the child, usually take a photo opportunity for parents and share a biker word of promise.

Since I have been back on my bike, I have taken many adventures. In only 12 months I have taken trips to Nevada, Utah, Idaho, New Mexico, Texas, Arizona, Colorado, Virginia Beach, North Carolina and Mexico. Only to return to some of these states multiple times due to befriending fellow bikers.

Leaving my mark everywhere I go you can be sure of three things with me:

1) I will talk and include everyone around me if they are open to receive.

2) I appreciate kids of all ages and will always stop to talk with them and their parents about riding a motorcycle.

3) I will always do my best to have a powerful message. And I love to use analogies according to a situation for easy remembering and to share a quote that will inspire. The simplest and easiest to remember. "If you rise, you might as well shine."

To know me is to know what it is to witness a woman given a second chance and with it, I love life and people. I embrace each moment that I am given, and I love to share it.

Today I actively live out a life of giving back - from which I once so selfishly took. I experience each opportunity to the fullest. I want to share with the next generation my belief. Understanding the importance and motto of the sisterhood of female riders: That we are a sisterhood always there for each other, not to harm but to hug, not to be mean but to lift up, not to destroy but to build, not to look away but to help. We all come from different backgrounds, but we all ultimately want the same thing, to be accepted and loved unconditionally.

To have a spiritual awakening and clarity like no other, I have hungered to ride for both pleasure and purpose. There are so many great causes out there that if I were able, I would do them all. But my absolute favorites are the ones that I get to interact and participate hands-on.

– Caroline Gordon rides a 2015 Road King.

Meet Caroline Gordon, aka Muminator. She is an inspirational speaker and Esthetician specializing in Oncology Aesthetics. Caroline currently lives in California. She tells us she, "enjoys riding her 2015 Road King out to the desert to watch a sunrise and head to the coast to catch a sunset, all on the same day." Caroline has made riding with a passion and purpose, her goal. Trying to bring inspiration to women and young girls who come into her life, she wants to leave a positive lasting impression.

DAWN - LAST RIDE

My best friend passed away in January in 2005. When she passed away, I was devastated. We were twin sisters of different mothers, and she literally took my secrets to the grave. We had been friends since the late 70's and rode on the back of motorcycles for years. Health issues eventually prevented her from riding. She supported my choice to get my motorcycle, which was a 2002 Dyna Glide I named Bluebob. She loved it when I would ride it over and rev it up just to show her neighbors she was still a biker.

Her sisters had given me some of her ashes in a beautiful little urn, and I thought the best way to honor our friendship was to take her with me on my rides. She loved to travel but had not been able to for a while. In April of the same year, I bought my second motorcycle, a 2006 Road King, I of course named Redbob. I tucked her away in one of my accessory bags, and away we went. I planned to spread her ashes along the way. A little here and a little there. We rode through several states in the Midwest, the Southwest, and all over Washington State. I had thought that when I took a trip that brought me to the Grand Canyon, that she would have wanted me to let her go there. But nope, I kept forgetting her at every beautiful destination I stopped at. So I settled with, she just is not ready to stop riding.

The next year I had another friend fly in from Alaska with the ashes of her longtime friend, Dennis. She and her husband rented a Harley, and we proceeded to ride to Mt. Eleanor in the Cascade Mountain Range of Washington State. I think it was about twenty miles or so of uphill gravel road. Not my favorite type of road! Other friends of Dennis were there to hike his ashes to the top while Norma, her husband, and I caught up on our lives.

The hiking party returned about an hour later with the rest of the ashes in tow. They were supposed to spread all of the ashes, but I think the final salute of whiskey took over before the task was completed. My friend turned to me with that look of desperation on her face and asked: "Do you want some of him?" She hadn't planned on returning to Alaska with him. Of course being the loyal friend how could I say no. But what to put some of him in. I remembered I had a medicine bottle with ten dollars worth of quarters in my saddlebag. I emptied the quarters into the bottom of the bag and turned to scoop some of Dennis into the medicine bottle. I then placed him next to my best friend Dawn and quipped "There 'ya go...I just found you a boyfriend."

They both rode with me on many adventures for a few

years until an opportunity came up. I had a friend with a place on the Big Island of Hawaii, and he had asked if I wanted to join him. I couldn't pass it up as that is the one place my best friend and I were planning to go before she died. I thought it a perfect place to let them both go together. Before we arrived on the island, I had made arrangements to rent a Harley while there. I put Dawn and Dennis promptly in the saddlebags of a light blue Harley Streetglide, which I dubbed Rent-A-Bob. We rode all over the Big Island. When it came time to let them go, we stopped at a makeshift bar on the way to the New Black Beach for the last drink and a photo op. This beach is being newly formed by the volcanic activity nearby. It was a little hike to the beach and well worth it. It opened up to beautiful rocks and glorious crashing waves. Perfect I thought, and I felt my best friend was pleased too. Another photo op of the two of them on the rock and I hung over the rock and emptied them both onto to the beach just slightly below. Farewell my friend and your boyfriend...it was a great ride.

Just a note to this story...a couple of years ago my best friend's son passed away, and his wife gave me some of his ashes. He now rides in my windshield bag along with a gal from Florida who rode a Spider motorcycle and passed from cancer. They both are sharing my riding adventures on my next Harley; a 2012 Streetglide named the "Red Dragon." It is comforting knowing I'm really not riding alone.

– Belinda Redbob she currently rides a Harley Streetglide

Meet Belinda Redbob. She had her first ride on a motorcycle when she was about six years old. It was a Harley from the 50's. She rode on the tank with her leg over the warm carburetor, and she says they went fast. She was hooked then. She had two uncles who rode motorcycles and several cousins who ride.

Belinda worked for a court as a Bailiff for over twenty years but decided to step back a bit and remain their best and only researcher. She says that working with criminals is very stressful. So she rides her Harley Streetglide that she named the "Red Dragon" because of the fairing. She says that "He has a whip I like to think of as his tail. It wraps and unwraps around my arm while riding. I have never seen anyone else's whip do this." Belinda has ridden in most of the states including Alaska and Hawaii, except the east coast. She even rode from Anchorage to Haines Junction Canada. She says when she rides she feels like she is dancing in the wind.

LOVING SUPPORT

"You will never become what you want to be, do what you want to do, or achieve your dreams without the support of those around you. Keep dreaming, keep driving, and keep pursuing your passion. The right people will surround you and those people will love nothing more than to see you succeed!" —Nicki Snyder, Editor

My first experience with a two-wheeled motorized vehicle was my brother's dirt bike. I begged to be allowed to ride it. Finally he relented and let me try. He gave me instructions on how to ride it and let me go. It was not until I got back that I realized he forgot to tell me how to stop. I let off the gas and jumped off the dirt bike. I broke it. Needless to say that was the last time he let me ride it. It was not until years later when I passed a woman riding a motorcycle that I felt that pull again. That feeling that I needed to ride my own motorcycle. It is funny that even with that feeling I did not do anything about it until a co-worker said she would take the class to learn to ride if I did it with her. I took the class, and the rest is history. Well... almost. I learned to ride but I still didn't have the confidence to ride on the road with cars. My husband, wanting to support me in my new sport, offered to follow me in our SUV while I rode my motorcycle. He did that for me for several days so that I could get comfortable riding on the road with all the cars and trucks. I think it is safe to say that if it was not for the support of my friend and husband, I may still have my license but would not have the experiences that shaped my love for riding my motorcycle.

– Sarah Andreas

STILL MAKING WONDERFUL MEMORIES TOGETHER

As the 2017 summer fast approaches it's end, it brings a flood of wonderful adventures memories!

In the early 1960's there were two little girls who were fortunate to make wonderful memories together. My cousin Sue and me. Our fathers were first cousins and great friends. The two of us spent many weekends and holidays together. Then life happened. My family moved and we were no longer nearby one another. Miles put distance between us, leaving only visiting opportunities at family events and funerals.

In 2007, Sue's father passed away. Once again we were able to visit one another. This time it was different. She and I were catching up on life's events and low and behold we both had BIG news. We both had recently purchased motorcycles and through talking realized ironically we had purchased the exact same bikes! We each had a Honda Shadow 600. We agreed this had to be some sort of a sign. The evening we figured all this out, we hugged and promised someday we would ride together. This gave us something to think about as we headed back to our respective homes in Missouri. Keep in mind, at this time we were both in our 40's and only had ridden on the back of motorcycles!

In 2009, the day came and we were finally ready to ride together. My husband was our trip adviser and lead bike. He planned a trip to the Tail of the Dragon. This was where the adventures began. Since that wonderful and eventful trip we have ridden to Maine, Canada, The Blue Ridge Parkway, New Orleans, Pikes Peak, Mount Washington (yes, we rode up and back down the mountain), Yellowstone, Glaser National Park, Niagara Falls, Grand Tetons, Arcadia Nation Park, oh, of course Sturgis and Orange County Choppers. I feel words can't describe our relationship or the beauty of the wonders of this earth!

Now we have both moved on from our Honda's and are on Harley-Davidson Heritage Softails. Imagine that, on the same bikes again! I am sure Sue will agree what we enjoy the most is being together and making wonderful memories together. As we approach a milestone of 60 years old, we have no intention of putting away our biking boots!

We welcomed Susan's honey to our little group. He mentions all the time how Sue and I are wonderful together. He can see our excitement through our tan faces and sunglasses. We certainly hope we can influence other ladies not to be afraid of the venture, but to respect their ride and the road. This is why Susan and I Ride!

– Vickie Barred currently rides a Harley-Davidson Heritage Softail.

Meet Vickie Barred, she is retired from the Schools for Severely Handicapped. Currently she works as a Weight Watchers Leader and Personal Coach. She and her husband have four sons between them. They have fourteen grandchildren and one great-grandson. She loves to ride as I am sure you can tell from her story. She didn't learn to ride until she was 47 years old. Her boys thought she had lost her mind. She says it was a huge challenge for her and she refused to give up. She also enjoys sewing, which she taught herself with the help of YouTube. Making children's quilts are her favorite. She lives in the beautiful Ozarks and enjoys day rides in the curves and twists of the road. She and her husband try to ride at least one day a month in the winter, which she admits can be a challenge.

LIVE LIFE

I had been on the back of my husband's bikes for a number of years. I loved the feeling of riding and wanted to ride my own. One year I was ready to take the safety course. I was two courageous mouse clicks away from registering for the course when I chickened out. Logic kicked in. I didn't have a bike to ride so I wouldn't be able to practice after I had my endorsement. We couldn't afford a bike for me and my husband's bike was too much bike for me to handle right away. The desire was there and I couldn't wait for my turn but the timing wasn't right for our house.

We went to Sturgis, South Dakota, for the annual rally in 2015. I felt like I was at home while we were there. I loved hearing and watching the bikes. The constant thunder of the engines was soothing. As we walked down one of the roads, I saw a group of women ride in. Those women were doing what I wanted to do. They were riding and experiencing life like so many others do, and so many other women want to do. I wanted to be one of them. Standing on that street corner, I felt like a little kid watching a parade saying, "When I grow up I want to ride a motorcycle just like them."

That night we got back to our room, I told my husband that I wanted to learn to ride. He didn't question it but simply said "Okay. Let's get you a bike."

The 2015 Sturgis Rally was a life-altering event in my life and inspired the tattoo on my left forearm that simply says "Live Life."

Six weeks after Sturgis we purchased a 2000 Yamaha V-Star 650 for me to learn how to ride. It had a slight oil leak that my husband was able to fix and it ran hot so I had to wear chaps each time I was on it. My supportive husband (now coach/riding instructor) rode the bike to a parking lot while I followed in the car. He taught me how to start it and how a manual transmission worked. He helped me pick it up when I dropped it and kept me going when I wanted to give up. Together we learned that the Yamaha could be run-jump started since I stalled it so many times the battery died. That Yamaha lived up to its primary role: a bike that it was okay to beat up a bit. My starter bike.

I earned my endorsement in May 2016 at the age of 39. The first time I took the Yamaha out on my own I made it half a block and stalled it at the stop sign for 15 minutes. I duck walked it across the intersection in my suburban neighborhood, turned it around, started it up and rode it the half-block home. I killed it in the driveway and had to push it into the garage while the neighbor (who also rides) watched everything on this first attempt. *How embarrassing!*

The second time I took it out I dropped it in a slow turn and my supportive husband had to come help me get it home. He fixed it up and I kept going the next week. The rest of my outings on the Yamaha went progressively better. I was able to do a couple small group rides by October 2016 for about 100 miles. One of my friends even got a picture of my husband and me on our bikes while we were at a stop sign. That picture is one of my favorite pictures ever because it showcases freedom, independence and support all in one quick snap.

I outgrew the Yamaha that season and bought my 2016 Harley-Davidson Softail Slim S just before the 2017 riding season. I named her Eleanor. Eleanor and I have been on 10,000 miles of adventures in our first year, all of them with my supportive husband by my side. We went to Texas Hill Country from Omaha, Nebraska two months after I got her home, including part of that trip on Historic Route 66. There were multiple trips to South Dakota where I rode Iron Mountain

Road and Needles Highway. The last adventure was my biggest accomplishment: I was one of the women riding her bike down the street in Sturgis during bike week. I was one of those women doing what so many others dream of doing: living life.
– Sarah Fisher rides a 2016 Harley Davidson Softail Slim S, "Eleanor"

Meet Sarah Fisher. She lives in Omaha, Nebraska and has an office job as an underwriter. She started riding a 2000 Yamaha V-Star 650 in 2015 then moved to a 2016 Harley Davidson Softail Slim S.

MIDLIFE PERSPECTIVE

To be honest, I had never given much thought to motorcycle riding. My experience of it had been limited to a few rides on a dirt bike on the farm we grew up on and a couple rides behind the dads of friends. Long drives have always been a great way for me to straighten out my thoughts.

Then, a little over five years ago, I met up with a guy I had known in high school. I had been a single, divorced mom of three for seventeen years and my hobbies were limited to the cheap or very free, stay-close-to-home-in-case-you-are-needed variety. That guy, my now husband, had ridden for years. At the time we got together he was without a motorcycle but he was so excited to really introduce me to riding that he rented a bike one day. That's when my motorcycle-riding journey began! It is humbling to realize that arthritis is making a very real appearance in our bodies and we have learned coping strategies such as taking frequent breaks to stretch our legs and taking good old ibuprofen before taking off.

We got married a little over three years ago at the local courthouse and decided we wanted to drive through town on our bike afterward, in our wedding gear. It was an extremely hot day in late June, and we made it out onto the street shortly after 3:00pm, meaning we were in the midst of rush hour traffic. We got a constant stream of smiles, congratulations, and honking horns. That is a pretty cool memory!

Once we got a bike of our own, I set out to obtain the proper gear. I am a nurse so I know the importance of safety. It makes me cringe to see young people riding with bare legs! I try to gently say something when I can. I planned to buy some used gear until I got used to wearing boots and leathers, and then eventually chose things more to my own liking.

I came across an ad on a local swap shop for a pair of Harley boots for sale in my size. The owner ended up being the mother of a boy that my three sons had played with frequently when they were young. She told me she had terminal cancer and the end was near so she would no longer be able to ride. I froze, not knowing how to react, knowing how much riding had meant to her. Because I had met her before, I decided to follow through with meeting her in person about the boots. She was beautiful and she had a joy and peace radiating from her that I have seen few times in my life. She was deep in her walk of faith. I have been sold out to Christ for years and found so much in common with her. Part of me wanted to apologize for buying the boots from her as she had loved riding so much. But in the course of our long conversation, she made me feel monumentally blessed, and I felt like she was passing along a baton to me of sorts, propelling me into a future of loving to ride motorcycles. She greatly expanded my awareness of Christian motorcycle riders. A few short months later, she passed away and I will never forget her. Her name was Debbie.

Due to family and work obligations, we have not gotten to go to as many bike rallies as my husband and I would like to. We were thrilled with our experiences at Daytona, Fayetteville, and Lake of the Ozarks. But we have also managed many jaunts in our state. I have been excited to find so many Christian sisters and brothers everywhere we go.

Recently, I was given a pair of Harley sunglasses from my daughter-in-law Karra. They had belonged her precious mother, Madonna, who unexpectedly passed away a few years ago within weeks of being diagnosed with cancer. It was a terrible loss for Karra, her sister, and the grandkids. But once again, we are not without hope, as Madonna was a Christian as well. I wear the sunglasses and my boots whenever I ride and I go forth into the wind and winding roads, praying I will be known as the loving, radiant, fun women both Madonna and Debbie were. I imagine the three of us in heaven, comparing our stories of riding. – Shelia Kable Mastalski currently rides a 2014 Harley Davidson triglide

Meet Shelia Kable Mastalski, she is in her mid-50's. She has three sons, two step-daughters and 14 grandchildren. She grew up actively participating in her family's farm in rural Centralia, Missouri. She was divorced for 17 years when I reconnected with someone who was a friend of mine in high school who became her husband and riding partner. She has been a nurse for over 31 years and also has a Bachelor's Degree in another field. She loves to learn new things and riding the beautiful countryside of Missouri.   Fun note: one of her granddaughter's first phrases was "Motorcycle! VROOOM!!!!" Her other Grandmother rides too!

THOSE 5 LITTLE WORDS

My husband has ridden a bike since he was 16, but I had always been a passenger. Being almost 6' tall, it was never a very comfortable ride for me as I was always looking for somewhere to stretch out my long legs. But I never dreamed of sitting in the "driver's seat… until that one morning about 18 years ago, when my "soon to be husband" and I were having breakfast with our parents. We were just having a normal conversation when I'm sure the conversation switched somehow to motorcycles. This has always been my husband's favorite discussion topic.

Out of nowhere, my future husband's mother asked my father if he thought I could ever ride my own motorcycle. My father's answer, "Yeah I'm sure she could." (My mother hated motorcycles until the day she passed by the way.) Up until that time, I had never even thought about riding "my own." Well, those five little words my dad spoke were all I needed. After that, as my husband says, "things started getting twice as expensive."

We bought a 1982 450 Nighthawk in 2001. I took it to my parents' backyard (they have about an acre of land), and my husband chased me around the yard screaming "IT'S NOT A DIRT BIKE!!!" I took the Motorcycle Safety Course, and at that time, you had to still go to the DMV to take the test. That Monday night after class, I broke my foot playing softball. I didn't get my license that year. So the following spring, I registered with a couple of friends to take the Motorcycle Safety Course again. I passed. One of the instructors had asked me if I would like to become an instructor. I looked at him like he had two heads. I was thinking, what could I possibly be able to teach anyone since I've only been on a bike for about two weeks total?

After a season of the Nighthawk, my husband bought his first Harley, a 2003 Electraglide Standard and he passed down his 1500 Vulcan Classic. I loved this bike, but it was NOT fuel injected and often, it would have carburetor issues. We sold that bike, and on the way home, we bought a brand new 2002 800 Vulcan which I owned for about nine years. I loved that bike as well, it "fit" me. After about nine years of riding that bike, I was itching for a Harley. I had always wanted a Harley, but my husband told me that I was not going to "wreck a Harley right out of the gate."

Eleven years later, I was finally able to get a Harley. We went to the Harley store in Cincinnati, and we were looking at Street Glides. I saw a few that I thought were nice – I knew I didn't want black and it had to be "used" to be in our price range. But then I saw "my bike." I noticed the price tag that was within our budget, so I went over to it and looked at it. It wasn't a color I would have "chosen" for myself, but it wasn't black either, so the price was right and the color wasn't wrong. It was a 2010 model, and I asked the salesperson how many miles were on the bike.

He said "16."

I said "Oh, 16,000?"

He said "No, 16."

I said "1600?"

He said "No, 16."

I said "Only 16 miles on this bike?"

He said "Yes."

I said, "What's wrong with it?"

As it turns out, this bike was a "raffle" bike. The person who won the contest did not want the bike; they wanted the money. That meant the bike came back to the dealer and had to be sold as a "used" bike. Well wasn't that just MY lucky day! So the color started to grow on me after that. I sat on that bike – while my husband continued to wander around the store. He came back and said, "I take it that's the bike you want since you have not gotten off of it since you got here?" I said "Yep."

About a week later, the Harley dealer delivered the bike to me on a snowy December day in 2010. I still have this bike.

About five years ago, one of my friends wanted to take the class. I told her I would take it with her. So we took it, once again, I was asked (this time by both instructors) if I wanted to be an instructor. Okay, this was the 3rd instructor that had asked me if I wanted to become an instructor. I had been riding 10+ years at this time, so I thought I would check into it. Four years ago, I became a Motorcycle Safety Instructor for the State of Ohio.

What a rewarding job. I love seeing students (especially women) who have never been on a bike before on Saturday morning to be a graduate Sunday afternoon. I have had many experiences with teaching in which I have been both humbled and in awe. I love watching the students' confidence build throughout the weekend.

In 2003, I became a member of the Motor Maids, one of the oldest continuous operating women's riding club in North America, established in 1940. Can you imagine a woman riding a motorcycle in 1940? And the criteria to be a member is you have access to a bike and "YOU ride." You cannot be a passenger in this club. And with this club, I have ridden many, many miles, and explored so much as you can only imagine on two wheels. And just think, this all started with five little words from my dad – "Yeah, I'm sure she could."

– Lori Rosenberger rides a Harley Davidson Street Glide.

Meet Lori Rosenberger, she lives in Ohio and has been married to Rob 16 years. They have hosted exchange students from both Germany (2012) and Luxembourg (2016) and are still in close contact with both students. Both students have been back several times to visit them. Lori and Rob also have a 4-year-old Shi-Poo named Jax. They named him Jax after the Jaxon Teller in Sons of Anarchy. Lori has a full-time job as a Systems Analyst with Procter and Gamble for almost 16 years. So she says, that she does not get to ride as often as she would like, but when she does ride, she makes it count. Lori is still a Motorcycle Safety Instructor for the State of Ohio, and loves to travel and vacation to new places. She says, "This world is huge, and I want to see it all. My motto is: I'll go anywhere or try anything once (except certain foods, I'll draw the line there) until it hurts or I figure out I don't like it. That way I get to experience the world!"

FIND THE ADVENTURE

The idea was spun on a whim. I've always enjoyed the ride, the scenery and the adventure but it wasn't until recently I thought I'd enjoy it any other way than on the back of my husband's Road Glide. After relocating our family to the Arkansas area, I started thinking "What if?" What if I learn to ride…What if I braved an obstacle… and What if I loved it? Taking those "what if's" and turning them into "why not's" were easier than I thought. No one would have imagined that my dreams would include getting my motorcycle license. In fact, many scoffed at the idea that I'd take a chance at my age with a family that needed me at home. The truth is age is just a number, and it didn't matter that I was fast approaching forty-one. Nor did it make any difference that I'm a wife and mother of three. Those factors don't define who I am or what I can accomplish they're just pieces of me as a whole. So without hesitation, I told everyone who would listen that this was exactly what I should be doing now. I've proven unequivocally that I can do anything I set my mind to, this should be no different. I am also very lucky that my husband encouraged me in my desire to join the ranks of women riders. Not once did he say you can't but constantly said, "You will."

As soon as I had the chance, I enrolled in the Harley Davidson New Riders course and anxiously awaited my class. That month was rampant with fear I couldn't do it to elation on challenging myself. The roller coaster of emotions anticipating the class had to be driving my husband crazy. He talked me through every doubt and celebrated my excitement. Then it was time, with four days to include classroom work and hours on the seat of the bike. I enjoyed meeting others in the same position I was with some varying experience. I would encourage anyone wanting to take this step to find a local riding course. They mentally prepare you for the adventure ahead and leave you with a little wisdom on what to expect. The instructors not only gave us practical knowledge but shared their own experiences with us. The course came and went with more ease than I had hoped for and gave me the confidence to do exactly what I had set out to do. Just this beginning step showed me how exciting my life was about to become.

My next adventure was finding the ride I was meant to have. The excitement of this stage was beyond anything I had ever expected. Scouring ads, looking at specs and narrowing down all my options. I worried about what was right for me too much, too little, seat height and handlebar reach. All those little details had me headed into a tailspin when we finally narrowed it down to two bikes. One was the bike I thought was what I needed with all the accessories and practicality. The other was the bike I dreamed could be mine with all its sleek style. Either bike would've made me a happy woman, but my husband swooped-in again to be my cheering section. Letting me know it was okay to catch the dream and enjoy my success. Within a week I had made my decision and was just waiting to bring my shiny new toy home. Nothing could've prepared me to pull into my driveway waiting for the garage door to finish raising and finding my bike sitting there. *Best gift ever!* My 2004 Harley Davidson Deuce is everything I had imagined and more. I love the growl of the pipes and the freedom it gives me. With all its beauty though came some insecurities that I couldn't handle it. Every time I take it out my confidence builds. I have goals, milestones and many hours in the seat ahead of me. Looking forward to the trips and bonding opportunities that my husband and I will have. I hope that anyone who has this desire to ride rises to the challenge. Learn to live and enjoy the open road...I know I am!

– Tara Sharp riding her 2004 Harley Davidson Deuce.

Meet Tara Sharp. She is 41 years old and currently lives in the Northwest Arkansas area. She has been married for 19 years and says her husband is amazing and they have three great kids. Tara works as an escrow assistant in a closing company.

40,000 MILES AGO

The grey winter clouds over Baden Wurttemberg simply added to my depressed state in the winter of 2010. The stress of sharing my two-bedroom apartment with my daughter, her significant other (that's a whole different story) and my granddaughter was manageable. The domineering nature of my boss had reached a tense pitch even after taking her to court on one occasion. Did I forget to mention my husband? He was in the apartment as well, off and on. It was only a couple weeks earlier that I had found a hotel receipt in his pants as I cleaned them out to wash. He denied that he was ever in that French town but could not explain the receipt. I may have overlooked that if I had not heard his telephone conversation with some woman that he took great care to make sure that I could not hear.

Then there was the day he left his phone within my reach after he had left the apartment. He denied, and to this day continues to deny, that he was with another woman. It was some years later that his denial somehow resulted in a child. As Christmas approached, I threw my third husband out of the apartment and felt the anxiety of being alone, cold, frustrated, embarrassed and used. I had only enough energy to tell my two daughters and two friends what had transpired.

I had only two close friends, Sybille and Bob. Sybille and I had become friends upon my arrival in Germany ten years earlier. Although older than my 52 years, she is a sweet lady with gypsy blood. Bob was an American and also older who I had met only five years earlier when he was working in the building next to my work. We saw each other several times standing outside smoking, he with his pipe and me with my roll your own cigarettes. As is often the case, our conversations were short, of no great consequence, but sufficient to become acquainted and find several areas of commonality.

Bob had completed his assignment in Stuttgart and returned to the U.S. a few weeks before Christmas. He left behind a girlfriend that he concluded he could live without rather than marry and bring her to the states. As she spoke no English and his Deutsch was no better than a third grader, I had met with them several times to translate. It was during those meetings and various times of Bob and I discussing our relationships that we became good friends who shared everything but sex. We had established that we were honest, open, and willing to take on any subject. When he returned to the U.S., I was left with only Sybille with whom I could be myself and express my feelings. As it was Christmas, I Skyped Bob to wish him a Merry Christmas. When we connected, he opened the door to me pouring out my anger and frustration. Expressing my need to get away, anywhere, he invited me to come to the U.S. I rejected that notion on many occasions when asked by other service members. But this time was different. It was not to visit the U.S. but to get away.

After telling my girls of this silly idea, they persuaded me to accept. Bob was in San Antonio, Texas for the winter. He had left his truck in North Carolina and instructed that I could only bring luggage that would fit on the back of his 2008 Harley-Davidson Ultra Classic...like I knew what that meant. We spent two weeks traveling in Texas and Louisiana, saw my first alligator and collected beads from Bourbon Street. I was able to experience the wind therapy that opened up an entirely new life for this country girl from Croatia. It was also during this visit that Bob and my relationship elevated to a whole new level. A level that prompted him to return to Germany to see if it would continue or if it was just the small head who had those feelings. It was on a subsequent visit to the U.S. that Bob took me to the Harley dealership in Charlotte, North Carolina. He enrolled me in the Motorcycle Safety Course and dropped me off to face my fears and doubts. At 450 kilo, I knew I would never be able to ride a big bike. Regardless, I wanted to feel the machine between my legs with me in control. Although I dropped the bike twice during practice, I passed the course even though I knew it had no influence on me getting an endorsement to my German driver's license. It did, however, accelerate my learning curve on the more challenging German course, which I passed later that summer. It was less than an hour after having my endorsement that Bob had me at the Stuttgart test riding a Harley-Davidson Fat Boy. Oh, it felt so good. I felt like a woman in charge of her future. That feeling faded quickly as Bob returned to the U.S. once again. It would be another five months before I would visit him again. I expected to be back on the rear seat, but that was okay. Until the day about a month before my arrival when he sent a picture of a Harley-Davidson 105th Anniversary Fat Boy. I was angry that he would taunt me so until he said it was sitting in his garage. The day after I arrived, he told me to pack a bag as we were riding to Daytona for Bike Week; some 500+ miles.

The bikes have changed to a 2012 Harley-Davidson Fat Boy and now a Harley-Davidson Road Glide Ultra. Ya, a big girl bike. Bob and I are now married, living in Florida and put 20,000 miles on the bikes from May to October this year. Many things have come together for me to change my life for the better. Bob's support and encouragement made it possible. The rest is all me.

— Mirjana Nichol, 2016 Harley-Davidson Road Glide Ultra

Meet Mirjana, *she is the third child of Stjepan and Zdenka Mavracic in Rugvica. She lived in the suburbs of the Jugoslavian (now Croatian* *capital). Upon graduation, Mirjana worked in the Jugoslovian National Bank. At 18, Mirjana married Branko and they had two girls, Ines and Ivana. After her divorce, Mirjana struggled as a single parent, so she left to work in Italy as an au pair, and after that, she worked in Stuttgart Germany as a telephone operator for the US military. In 2005 Mirjana met her current husband, Bob Nichol, who was assigned to European Command (EUCOM). Over the next four years, the couple's relationship emerged and they married in Hot Springs, South Dakota during the 2015 Sturgis Bike Week. Mirjana has five grandchildren. She regularly attends yoga and is actively perfecting her pottery skills. Mirjana enjoys motorcycle riding and golf. She devotes a great deal of time to buying and reselling antiques, collectibles, and memorabilia. Bob and Mirjana now live in Florida.*

A RESOUNDING, "YES!"

I am 65 years old and have been riding my Indian Scout for two years. Although I have had my motorcycle license since my early 20's, I had not ridden independently for 45 years. My husband has had several motorcycles over the years and I enjoyed being a passenger. A seed of inspiration was planted a few years ago when my sister-in-law, who is close to my age, started riding her own Harley Davidson 883 Sportster. My journey was decided, though, when I asked my husband if he would be comfortable with me on my own bike and he responded with a resounding, "Yes!" I decided to take the motorcycle safety class. When I entered the room the first day, the ageist male instructor told me, "The crocheting class is next door."

Undaunted by his words, I successfully completed the two-day class. I experienced a good deal of fear in my beginning days and months. I used to say that my 1100cc motorcycle had 1000cc more than I needed. But, as I gained more time in the saddle, that which used to intimidate me now exhilarates me! Speed, curves, traffic... I welcome it all. Last year I was thrilled to complete the Tail of the Dragon, twice actually, with 318 curves in 11 miles. I love taking my helmet off so people see my white hair and then contemplate my age. The world is full of people who will try to keep you in the box they have ascribed to you because of your age, gender or whatever. There are just as many who will support and encourage you to step outside that box. I am grateful to those people in my life: friends, family and the Internet biking community. I enjoy reading about older women who ride and continue to be inspired by their spirit. I hope to ride the wind for many years to come.

– Sherry Burdick, 2015 Indian Scout

Meet Sherry Burdick. She is 65 years old and has been riding her 2015 Indian Scout for two years. She is a retired school psychologist who lives in the upstate New York city of Oswego.

I SAY GO FOR IT.

I first started riding when I was 16 years old. My boyfriend at the time, who I went on to later marry, was a rider and would quite often pick me up on his bike (a DR 200 at the time). He taught me to ride on a Honda XR 100. I mostly went pillion with him though, as the 100 wasn't ours. It wasn't until a couple of years later that we acquired an older Honda XL 185. At the time it was a newer bike. That's when I went for my license. Thankfully, we lived in a rural area and didn't have to do the weekend courses to get my license. All I had to do was ride around the block while the tester watched. Surprise – I passed! But three months later was pregnant with my first child. Not long after that another little one came along. So I didn't really ride for about eight years.

After that season in life had passed, I decided to drag that XL 185 out of the shed and get it registered again. I was terrified riding the 3 km to the mechanics on the road with traffic on my own, I really had no experience with traffic. But I did it. I slowly started riding again. I still have that bike (it's nearly 30 years old). She's a bit of a wild ride these days, but it's an appropriate initiation for any of the kids wanting to start riding. If you can ride the XL, you'll probably be able to ride anything.

Over the years, I've had periods of riding frequently and had big breaks. It depends on what's happening in our lives.

Back in 2009, I tried to organize a ride for my husband's 40th birthday to the tip of Cape York. All of our friends that ride and would be capable of such a ride weren't interested. I thought: "I have my license, I ride off-road, there is no reason why I can't do something like that." So we did a three-day ride out of Cairns.

I ended up being the only girl with eight guys. I absolutely loved it! Riding off-road allows you to go places and see things that a lot of people miss out on, and tropical Queensland truly has some beautiful places to see. It was only three days, but it was a big experience for me. I went everywhere they went. I didn't have any laydowns. I will never be a fast rider, but I'm not competing and I don't hold up the group. As our tour guide said, slow riders don't slow you down, riders riding above their skills do. I rode through many rivers, including The Daintree River, wide and sandy, and walked my bike through a river with flowing thigh-deep water with a rocky base. I rode on the Creb track, which is an iconic trail amongst dirt bike riders and is known as one of the hardest 4wd tracks in Australia. It's very steep and rough. The slightest rain makes it treacherous. And I rode on it.

My husband and I are lucky enough to own 100 acres of land. We have a motor cross track plus a 3km boundary track. We also have access to state forest and a very large property next door where we can go for a 4-hour ride and still be on the same property. As our family has grown up and our friends' children as well, we have spent many weekends out at the property and had so many fun times.

All our children ride. They've all started on 50cc quads or peewee's. My 16-year-old daughter rides in the bush with us, and she rides very well. Always impressed by her riding skills, I can't keep up with her. Soon, she will have her license and be able to join us on longer rides. There are way too many times that we've gone on weekend rides using our property as a base camp. We have an event at our property once a year. Only for people we know. Our biggest Poker Run we had 60 riders. We've done it ten years in a row now. We give out trophies every year. It makes me so glad to see the next generation of riders growing up and we have quite a few young girls riding as well. I love encouraging them.

My best friend rides and together we have encouraged another friend to get her first bike as well. I thought I was doing well when I would go for a 10km ride without the boys, in the bush (that was ten years ago). I never thought I'd be doing the riding I do now. Now our friend is in that position. The only difference is if they took me the places we've taken her, with no experience at all, I would've given up. We are all so impressed that she hasn't.

I have come across a couple of blokes that seem to feel that off-road riding is just for the boys. But I'm not bothered by that attitude. Why should they have all the fun? Being able to ride off-road and being licensed has allowed me to do too many rides to count in groups and with my husband. I think having a hobby in common only strengthens a relationship. My husband and I are currently planning an overnight ride this weekend. We are going somewhere I have never ridden. I am so glad I took the time to get my license; it allows me to enjoy both road and trail. Although I definitely enjoy off roadway more, we can go places and see things that a lot of people can't. As our kids get older (our son is 19 and our daughter is 16), we get more and more free time. That time will definitely involve more riding. If you're a woman and tossing up whether or not to ride, I say go for it. Why not? What is stopping you? – Siobhan Zmegac rides a Suzuki DRz 250.

Meet Siobhan Zmegac, she is 41 and works in retail. Siobhan lives in Northern New South Wales, Australia. She rides a Suzuki DRz 250. At one point in their family of four, they had: a DRz 70, 125, 250, 400 and a 650. Now they have a Yamaha TT-r 230, Drz 250, 400, two 650's, XL 185, and a Kawasaki KXf 250. They certainly love their bikes!

INSPIRATION

"People often say that this or that person has not yet found himself.
But the self is not something one finds, it is something one creates."
- Thomas Szasz

KEEP YOUR PROMISES TO YOURSELF

My first moped was a Honda Urban Express, my second a red Honda Spree. In the mid-1980's a 49cc engine was enough to get me to high school and my various jobs. I envisioned a motorcycle for myself one day but could not justify it until I had accomplished a few things first. So I sold the moped in exchange for a Volkswagen.

At 20 years old I had skipped the college experience because the money was not available for me to attend so I entered the workforce and married my high-school sweetheart. The kids came along not long after and I became immersed in caring for my family. My two daughters played top-notch soccer and my life was filled with working and jockeying between practices, games and social schedules. Like many women, I set aside my own aspirations to lift up the ones around me.

After 18 years of marriage my husband and I split up, and a couple of years later I found I abhorred my job, my friends, my lack of participation in my own life and my alcohol addiction became more than I could handle on my own. In the middle of all of this, I married a lovely man who stood by me as I scraped bottom and worked to re-make myself. I quit my job. I focused on recovery. I did what I call, "hit reboot" on my life. I started running and also began my college education. I promised myself if I got my college degree, I would finally get that motorcycle I had always wanted.

I scooted around on my beloved 2001 Yamaha Zuma to buzz myself on and off campus, but I longed for more rumble under my seat.

I became president of our E-TV Club, a campus student organization focusing on television production. I made some of the best friends I've ever had in my life. After five years I was finally ready to graduate. In April of 2017, I graduated Summa Cum Laude, acquiring my Bachelor's of Science degree.

The very weekend after commencement I took the motorcycle endorsement class and passed. One week after that I bought my dream bike, a 1980's era Honda. There were less than 5,000 miles on this beauty!

With only about 200 miles of actual riding experience, I wrote my motorcycle into a film we made for a film competition…and it won five individual awards including "Audience Choice."

Roadmap allowed me both a writing and directing credit but I was most excited to get the Stunt Woman credit! To promote the film we made postcards, flyers, and t-shirts. It took me 48 years, but I had finally managed to get myself onto a t-shirt, an incredible silhouette of me on my motorcycle.

I continue to ride my Honda "Hank" when I need quiet time to myself. I named my motorcycle after the blue Beast character in X-Men. Anything with that much power between my legs must be male. I'm training for my seventh marathon, and even as I'm out training on the roads, I think of how it feels to have the ground pass by underneath my feet so much faster when I'm on Hank. My heart skips a beat every time that engine roars to life.

Getting that motorcycle endorsement on my license was a 30-year dream that finally came to be realized because I signed up. I sold that Yamaha Zuma on a Friday and used every penny of it to buy my Hank the following Monday. No one else rides it; it's mine. It feels incredibly indulgent because it is just for ME and that's one of the reasons I love it so much. Keep your promises to yourself. It's never too late to make good on them. – Heather V. Irvine, she rides her ride Honda named "Hank".

Meet Heather V. Irvine, she is 48-years-old and works as a Customer Service Specialist at R.E.I. in Ann Arbor, Michigan and lives in a neighboring town. She will become a grandmother in April of 2018 and could not be more excited or proud. She hopes to venture further with Hank, possibly embarking on a motorcycle trip of her own. In the meantime, she plans to work on her first screenplay. She says "I mean. . . Why not?" Link to her film Roadmap - https://youtu.be/_qTIl860vck

SOUL FULFILLMENT

"Just sitting in the garage remembering all the places I have visited over the last few years and how each has a story and how privileged I have been to be a part of that story. Just thinking about how riding is the ultimate Zen experience for me and how it heals and steals at the same time. Steals time and money and neither really matter in the end.
But healing, no matter how you do it, it matters."
– Facebook, October 18, 2017, Lynn Cromwell's personal page

Twenty-two years ago I had lunch with a girlfriend I had once worked with. At the end of the conversation, she happened to mention she was selling her motorcycle because her partner had bought her a bigger new bike for her birthday. On a whim, I said, "I'll buy it."

I had never been one of those people who dreamed of riding my whole life; this purchase was a gut response that changed my life in more ways than I ever dreamed could happen. I went home that afternoon and said to my husband at the time, "I hope you don't mind, but I bought a motorcycle today."

As a previous rider who gave it up for family reasons, he was more than enthusiastic about my purchase and went out that same week and bought himself a brand new motorcycle so we could ride together. Within two years I upgraded to a larger bike and we made plans for our first trip out West. This trip was three weeks and over 7,000 miles. I was smitten. Since that time, I have upgraded my bikes three times to be better able to do what I love, exploring North America. I have ridden coast to coast twice, once using a southern route and just this year a northern route through Canada. Currently, I have ridden in all of the contiguous states except for three and all of the southernmost Canadian Provinces.

Ten years into my riding experience I became a Motorcycle Safety Foundation (MSF) instructor. I have a lot of certifications and a couple degrees from different sources, which means I have gone through numerous types of training for my career in leadership development and training and also as a mental health therapist. But never had I experienced the rigor of the motorcycle instructor training class. We started the first weekend with 33 students, of which only three were women. The second weekend there were 16 students left, and I was the only woman to make the cut. It was tough and well worth the work. I think all of my work makes a difference, but I love walking into a classroom of students eager to start the journey that has given me such fulfillment.

As a mental health therapist, I am often asked how I

separate myself from my work. Riding, planning a ride, and remembering a ride all bring me peace. The people I meet remind me of the kindness that is still available in abundance and how your openness to it matters. This is one example out of the many I stories I could tell you.

On my first ride coast to coast, Connecticut to California, we chose a southern route in mid-July and August. We stopped at a rest stop for water and a break in New Mexico where the temperatures danced in the lower 100's. Unfortunately, there were no vending machines and the 'only drink from if you absolutely have to' water fountains were broken. A woman noticed our blight and asked if we needed water. We said yes and we would pay if she had some available. She told us not to be silly, she had plenty and it was really cold. She led us to a vehicle hauler where she was hauling three oversized vans and loaded us up with crackers with peanut butter and cookies and ICE COLD WATER. She and my partner exchanged road knowledge and some similar experiences as he has driven eighteen-wheelers and soon we were back on the road, refreshed and ready for the next hundreds of miles. This woman was one of the many angels we have met on the road. I know many bikers hate riding with truckers but not me. As a group, I have found truckers to be the ones looking out for us and I respect them and the work they do.

I have recognized when I come back from a ride of a few thousand miles or more that all the pieces of me have been aligned. At the end of the day, when I want to reconnect with myself, I choose to ride. When I want to recoup from a day, week or year, I choose to ride. When I feel like I am alone on this earth, I choose to ride. When I want to be alone on this earth, I choose to ride. I guess as long as these two legs can hold up those two wheels, I choose to ride.

— Lynn Cromwell rides a 2017 Harley-Davidson Street Glide

Meet Lynn Cromwell, LMFT from Connecticut. She purchased her 2017 Harley-Davidson Street Glide in July of 2017. And as of October 5, 2017, she has 10,100 miles on it. She is the mother of 2 children, 2 dogs and grandmother of 7. She is employed at Total Balance Center, LLC., a small mental health therapy office in Marlborough, and is an Adjunct Professor at both the University of Hartford and Central Connecticut State University. She also teaches for the Motorcycle Safety Foundation as a rider coach for the State of Connecticut.

A SPIRITUAL JOURNEY

"I want to inspire and empower women throughout the world, and hope that they too, can face their fears, tackle head-on any daunting challenges in front of them. To be an example of what it means to replace fear with love and allow oneself to follow our dreams, whatever they may be."
-Ruth Blecher

India, where could I possibly begin? For as long as I can remember, I have always wanted to see the Taj Mahal. I first learned about it in grade school, I was so fascinated by its beauty and architecture. I never dreamt that I, a little girl from Price Hill (small neighborhood in Cincinnati, Ohio), would ever be able to go to such a place, so far away.

When I first heard about the Moto-Expedition led by Tiffany Coates (world's foremost solo motorcycle female rider) in 2014, I could hardly contain my excitement. I was excited to be part of a women's ride to "The Highest Motorable Road in The World, Khardung-La (18,380 Feet)."

I've been riding since I was about 10 years old. I learned how to ride on a Kawasaki KE-100 and Suzuki DS-80. Growing up, I was very adventurous and loved to ride everywhere, on my grandparent's 7-acre farm, through the strip-coal mines of the Kentucky Appalachians, in the sand and dirt of the California desert and mountains.

This ride, however, was going to be different. I was 49 -- about to turn 50, I was 160+ lbs., overweight, and if I expected this to be a successful trip, I needed to make some very serious changes in my life. In many ways, my life had been stifled by fear. I was so paralyzed by my fear of flying; it deprived me of exploring the world. Even though I had obstacles to overcome, they would not stop me-- I was going to India.

I started exercising -- walking, swimming, racquetball and dieting. Of course, I had a few setbacks over the months to come but before I left, I lost about 45-50lbs and another 20lbs thereafter. I also prepared and conditioned my body by riding off-road and attending local rallies and rides in the weeks and months beforehand. One particular day I decided I would practice water-crossings with a few friends. I knew that there would be water-crossings in India and I really needed to over-come my fear of them, so... I did.

I fell in love with the Royal Enfield Bullet-500. The style was classic and it is such a beautiful bike. Mine was the only carbureted engine and had road tires. I was convinced these tires would not be sufficient to ride off-road, especially in the Himalayas! I was totally wrong; it was amazing despite the road conditions. I absolutely love it. It was not all that comfy when hitting bumps or potholes at higher speeds but handled very well.

The trip really started to come to life for me when we arrived in Manali. When Tiffany said, "Manali is the gateway to the Himalayas," it absolutely took my breath away.

The ride was amazing on so many levels. It did not hit me until we rode through the twisties outside of Kelong, that I was finally in the Himalayas. Once the mountains opened up, I was overcome with emotion and started to weep in my helmet, the tears just streamed down my face -- it was so majestic, the valleys were splattered with colors of greens, purples, greys and the lakes were jade.

As we approached the Tibetan Plateau, the switch-backs were frequent and the hairpin turns often steep, ascending and descending. The roads were carved out of the Himalayas with the occasional granite canopy, the drop-offs are not like anything I've ever seen before. As we rode through the valleys, roads were often rough, rocky, deep gravel, sandy, and wash-board surfaces. The road along the Chandra River was unpaved, muddy, pitted and I loved every minute of it. There would be vistas that I would come upon or rock formations that would just send chills through my spine, this would be a trip I would never forget.

Many times at the end of the day, I felt like I had become an adrenaline junkie. For the first time in my life, I am totally living in the moment. The chaotic driving and overtaking of vehicles in unimaginable terrain was exhilarating.

This trip was motivated by my passion for motorcycling, my deep desire to follow a dream, to see the Taj Mahal and ride a motorcycle through the Himalayas.

I fell in love with the Indian people, food and culture. I was deeply moved by the poverty and horrified by the masses that were homeless. India is a nation of peace, love and kindness – I experienced that every day.

I went to India with an open heart, mind and spirit. This was not just a motorcycle expedition – it was a spiritual journey

and it changed my life.
— Ruth Belcher rides Yamaha V-Star 1100

Meet Ruth Belcher, she is the Founder of Global Moto Adventures, LLC, an organization dedicated to empowering women to follow their dreams of motorcycle travel, inspiring one another to build a community of like-minded souls by creating opportunities for connection and promoting the annual Pacific Northwest female-centric event, Flock to the Rock. Born in Cincinnati Ohio, Ruth has been a wanderer at heart from an early age. She first started riding motorcycles around age nine and got her first bike a year later, a Suzuki DS80. Ruth purchased a cruiser, Yamaha V-Star 1100 and started riding locally with other women riders. Ruth then went on an epic solo ride through 10 western states, 4,800 miles, 21 days. This ride was life changing for Ruth, but she knew something was missing — dirt, her first love. Ruth then began her search for just the right bike to become the Adventure Rider she is today. Ruth had a dream to one day see the Taj Mahal and ride a motorcycle through the Himalayas so she put in motion, a life altering trips through the northern region of India and Pakistan. You can check out her Facebook page at
https://www.facebook.com/GlobalMotoADV/

RIDE OF MY LIFE

I rode mini-bikes as a kid. I had a Rupp and my brother P.J. had a Hodaka. A lot of fun times, crashes and laughs spent on country fields. No helmets or safety gear. How did we survive? It was a different time it seems. Fast-forward many years when my husband and I got married, had three babies and life moved on. My husband Joe has always ridden motorcycles, from a Yamaha IT 200 to an FJ 1200 to a Honda Shadow. He always had in the back of his mind one day he'd like to own a Harley Davidson. Years later in 2012, after the kids were grown, his dream became a reality. He bought a brand new, beautiful black Harley-Davidson Switchback from a dealer in Syracuse, NY. We rode a year on that bike together, enjoying every second. He kept encouraging me to take a ride on my own, just a short jaunt around a parking lot. He kept saying how much he thought I would love it. Long story short, I DID ride around a couple times and oh boy did it feel amazing! That Fall, he found an 1999 Harley-Davidson 883 Sportster Hugger model for me. It had forward controls and was the perfect size for beginner. I was super-psyched.

My husband had the patience of a saint when I was learning to ride. He taught me how to maneuver twists and curves and make turns AND have confidence when I ride. He spent several months driving slow and taking back roads practicing with me. He taught me to do a Figure 8 and to always be two steps ahead of others on the road. He never rushed me or became frustrated. By that summer, I was ready to take my driving exam. I passed! It was an exhilarating feeling when I rode my bike home that day. I enjoyed my "Sporty" for almost a year and by the following summer was ready to go bigger. I bought my first brand new Harley-Davidson in 2014, an Amber Whiskey Switchback. My kids were texting me the minute the new line came out because my favorite color is orange and I had said to them if Harley-Davidson made a new color that year I was getting one. And that's exactly what I did! It was one of the best decisions I've ever made.

My husband and I put many miles on the bikes that following summer. I was feeling awesome and totally in control of my own bike. When the new line came out the next year, my husband fell pretty hard over the new Road Glide Special. After a test ride, he was sold and bought one that day. I continued to ride my Switchback until that Fall when I test drove a Street Glide Special...and I guess you can figure out the rest. I bought one, another Amber Whiskey. That bike was very popular that year and the one I bought was actually the last one in the State of New York. We found the bike at a dealer way up north in Adams Center. My husband wanted me to have it all...stage one air cleaner and exhaust, Vance & Hines true duals, auxiliary lights, chrome customization and heated hand grips too. He even surprised me and had the dealer install electro glow lighting on the front fairing!! I could hardly wait to throw my leg over the seat. It was March when I picked her up, so a balmy 30 degrees outside that day. I HAD to take her for a short snort around the lot. It felt magical! I put over 8,000 miles on my bike that first year and we only have four to five months of good riding in New York!

Fast-forward again to the present, we've traveled over 50,000 miles on our bikes since 2012 and found each time better than the last. We've seen mountains and oceans, forests and landscapes whose beauty can only be appreciated actually being there. I remember driving through West Virginia this past summer, through the George Washington National Forest and thinking to myself: "I am the luckiest person alive; I am seeing ALL this incredible beauty and on my Harley Davidson motorcycle!"

It just doesn't get any better! We have hopes to travel cross-country from New York to Montana for our 30th wedding anniversary.

My husband has been my greatest friend, not only in riding but in life. He makes me feel like I am the very best at all I do. He is my ride or die and I know God blessed my life by giving him to me. Likely I never would have had the opportunity or the desire to ride my own motorcycle had I not had his encouragement. Our riding is like our love story. We go together, have each other's backs and ALWAYS look forward to the next adventure.

– Shelley Wyman rides a 2015 Harley Davidson Street Glide Special.

Meet Shelley Wyman. Besides her Street Glide Special, she also owns a 1999 Harley Davidson 883 Sportster, Hugger model. Her husband Joe rides a 2015 Harley Davidson Road Glide Special. Shelley sent a photo of her and her husband sitting side by side on motorcycles, holding hands. You can see it on our Facebook page:
https://www.facebook.com/womenwhoridebook She says, "The photo says it all for me. My husband Joe has been by my side since I was 13 years old when we started dating, he was 16. We were together all through high school and college and were married in 1990. We've since been together 27 more years. It's been the best ride of my life."

EMPOWERED & PROUD

When life begins again at 53. I've been married 31 years. I have watched my children and grandchildren grow. All while having a successful career as a nurse that abruptly ended after a horrible allergic reaction. I spent the next 11 years extremely ill, died three times, had two tracheotomies, feeding tubes and an immune deficiency. When my health began to improve my husband and I vacationed in Hawaii and that's where my love for riding began!

In February of 2017 in Hawaii, we rented scooters and had an absolute blast! I told my husband I wanted to get one. Coming back to California, I took the MSF class in April and told my husband I was ready for a motorcycle. After he got over the shock and was able to process and realize my full desire, we purchased my first bike on May 12, 2017!

I was nervous, scared and at times terrified thinking "you're 53 years old…are you crazy?"

But I prayed, talked about it with my husband and sent my bike pictures to my kids. I got all kinds of "OMG" responses! In the five months since then, I have practiced, pushed myself, dropped my bike twice and got right back on. Most of all I have completely enjoyed myself and love riding every chance I get. I have put 7,000 miles on my "SuzyQ" and everyone that knows me has told me since I've had my bike they've seen me sparkle, become more confident on/off the bike and even become healthier. My husband always tells me I'm making up for lost time. I've ridden with three charities so far. I am in the process of joining a Women's Motorcycle Club and took my longest solo ride of almost 1200 miles!

I rode from Northern to Southern California and again thought I was crazy! But at the same time I felt so free, empowered and proud riding along the freeway, coastal and mountain roads. My biggest fears were being alone, hitting roads that had horrible conditions which scared the crud out of me and facing rain and hail which I discovered really hurt when riding! Overall, it was the best experience and I can't wait to do a trip soon to Oregon.

I could never imagine not riding and totally enjoy every minute on the road, especially seeing other women riding! I love the camaraderie of other bikers on the road and feel such pleasure when I give the biker wave. Instead of my life ending at 53, I feel my life has just begun again. You're never too old and it's never too late to ride!

– Teri DeLaCruz rides a 2003 Honda Shadow Spirit 750 M

Meet Teri DeLaCruz, she is a wife, mother of three girls and grandmother of five boys. She is a Disabled/Retired Registered Nurse and rides a 2003 Honda Shadow Spirit 750 M. She is from California.

COURAGE IN THE FACE OF FEAR

I grew up riding horses but had never ridden a motorcycle until I was an adult. The first time I rode on one was in 2010 when a friend was selling a red Ducati, and my husband was interested. I rode with my friend to see if I would like it or not. Even though my forearms hurt from holding on tight out of fear, I was immediately in love! It was like galloping at full speed on a horse who never got tired! My husband bought the bike, and once he got his license, I was riding with him every chance I got.

After only a few summers riding with my husband, I decided I was sick of waiting around for him to ride and wanted to be able to ride myself. Plus he, his daughter, and I couldn't get all ride together. I also struggled with staying awake on the back with him on longer rides. He is a very safe rider, so soon I wasn't afraid and sometimes would start to doze off. A few times it was so bad that my helmet hit the back of his jacket before I was able to let him know we needed to pull over!

My husband insisted that I get at least a 650 since we live out in the country and do a lot of highways and interstate riding and he wanted me to be able to keep up with traffic to be safe. We went looking for bikes, and I saw a bike that looked small enough that I might be able to learn to ride on it without killing myself. It was a beautiful blue, my favorite color, with a matching blue spring looking thing that I learned later was a shock. It was a 2009 ER6N, and it was love at first sight. It is the bike that I still ride today.

Next was the challenge of learning to ride. I was afraid to take a class at first because I was terrified that I would be the only woman and would be intimidated by all of the guys there who I assumed would know way more about riding then I did. My husband said that he could teach me, and boy did he ever try. But either he is an awful teacher, or I am a terrible student! Let's just say that I got very good at not getting trapped under my bike while tipping it over! This was my fear, and I didn't have faith in my ability to keep it upright. So after probably five times of tipping it over, mostly at stop signs or while doing very slow turns, I finally gave up and signed up for a class.

In the class, I took there was one other woman with me as well as some teenage boys and the rest were men. No one else knew how to ride either- imagine that! I had butterflies in my stomach, and I remember saying a lot of prayers. I told myself that I could quit anytime I wanted, but I really wanted to learn how to ride, so I didn't give up. We got to use little 250 bikes that were much easier to learn on. I never tipped one of their bikes over the whole class or in the driver's exam for my license. I have never tipped over on a bike since.

A few years ago while riding with my husband at night, shortly after we turned on to a side highway, my husband slowed down, and I realized why when I saw some deer running along the right side of the road. We have a lot of deer in our area, and unfortunately, a lot of car and motorcycle accidents happen each year involving deer. I stopped as quickly as I could but before I completely stopped one of the smaller deer darted in front of me. I remember looking over my handlebars to see the deer and then the impact. I was able to keep my bike up and sat stunned while the deer must have run off into the woods. After a minute I realized I was stopped in the middle of a windy, dark highway. I pulled over to the side, and we checked out my bike. My headlight was cracked, but it still ran so I got right back on and rode home. Once I got my bike repaired, I was right back to riding.

I have been riding for four years on my own. I put more miles on my bike than my husband puts on his every season.

We have gone on a few longer trips together including a ride up to Copper Harbor, Michigan, but mostly I commute to work and go on weekend rides. The death grip I had on the handlebars my first month of riding is long gone, and I have to remind myself to slow down a lot of the time. I got pulled over for speeding this past summer but only got a warning. I think the officers were surprised when I removed my helmet to find a female rider. That is a response I often get from people.

I have struggled with fear and anxiety a lot of my life and with them often comes the temptation to stick with what is comfortable and easy and avoid trying new things. Riding didn't come easily to me at first and took a lot of courage and determination. This is one of the things I absolutely love about it. Every time I get on the bike I am reminded how strong and courageous I can be. I am reminded that when I ask for help, practice determination, and have some faith, I can accomplish whatever God asks of me or blesses me with. I hope that when I share my story with others, it inspires them as well.
– Arianna Saykally-McAdams rides a 2009 ER6N.

Meet Arianna Saykally-McAdams. She grew up in Nebraska and currently lives in Minnesota. She is a psychotherapist working with children and adult survivors of sexual abuse/sexual assault. Arianna likes to ride her 2009 ER6N sports bike from her home to Winona, Minnesota or to work in Onalaska or Prairie Du Chein, Wisconsin. She is married to Gabe, and she has a stepdaughter, Kaitlyn, who enjoys riding on the back of her dad's bike.

TAKE CONTROL OF THE HANDLEBARS OF YOUR LIFE

It was 1995, and I was active duty Air Force assigned to Davis Monthan Air Force base in Tucson, Arizona. My husband of nine years decided he was going to buy a Harley. I was riding on the back with him and felt that wind in my face and that freedom and thought: "I want to learn how to ride a motorcycle."

For any military member who wants to ride a motorcycle, it is mandatory to take the Motorcycle Safety (MSF) Course. Now, the MSF Course is many hours of professional coaching/training over several days. Professional coaching equals professional results! I signed up for the course and couldn't get in for a couple of months.

In the meantime, I found this beautiful 883 Harley Davidson Sportster. It was a deep maroon color. I bought it, and my husband rode it home. I walked by it in the garage looking at it longingly, and I'd sit on it and imagine the adventures I'd have and the places I'd go. I didn't know how to ride. There are so many different things going on when you ride a motorcycle. One down, 4 or 5 up? What the heck does that mean? Plus, you have to figure out what to do with your hands and feet, and you are in sensory overload because you are in the open and not surrounded by a car.

Despite the fact that I was apprehensive and kind of afraid to learn, I was ready to take the course and anxious to learn.

One day, my husband decides he's going to teach me how to ride... Lesson Number One! Do NOT, never ever, EVER under ANY circumstances let someone who is not a trained motorcycle rider coach teach you how to ride a motorcycle!

It was a beautiful warm and sunny day. My husband backed the motorcycle out of the garage, down the driveway and into the street. He proceeds to give me a whole five minutes of instruction on how to ride a motorcycle. Whether you want to learn how to ride a motorcycle or achieve your dreams in life, you need professional coaching. Professional coaching equals professional results. Limited coaching equals limited results. Let me give you an example of limited coaching...

At this point in my life, I couldn't drive a stick shift car. I didn't own a stick, couldn't drive a stick, and that whole clutch thing was kind of beyond me. There I am, sitting on the bike and he's telling me how the clutch, throttle and shifter work in about five minutes. When he was done, I was more confused than when he first started and a little afraid but I grabbed the handlebars anyway and got ready to ride.

Then, he hops on the back! Lesson Number Two! Do NOT, never ever ever under any circumstances ride somebody on the back of your motorcycle until you've had at least six months to one-year riding experience. Especially not a 6 foot 200-pound man that outweighs you almost 2 to 1. Why? Adding more weight changes the whole center of balance of the bike, you need to be an experienced rider before you attempt this.

There we are, going around the block. My hands are on the handlebars but so are his. I think I'm in control, but he's really in control.

How many times do we do that? We think we're in control, but somebody else is doing the steering. We can't reach the handlebars of life because we've given control to somebody else...

We circle the block a couple more times and stop in front of the house which brings me to Lesson Number Three. Do NOT, never ever, EVER under any circumstances even attempt to ride a motorcycle until you understand it's operation and how it works.

What happens when you let out the clutch? It starts to roll forward... I let out the clutch; the thing starts to roll forward, it freaks me out. I roll hard on the throttle, and it shoots out from under me like a patriot missile and hits the ground with this horrible crunching sound. I fall off; he hops off, I run into the house screaming, "Forget it! I quit! Sell the bike!"

He rolls the bike back into the garage. Despite the horrible crunching sound, it only had a ding in the tank, the clutch lever and turn signal were broken and a couple of other minor dings. At this point, you couldn't even get me to look at the bike! I walked past it in the garage with blinders on.

For months I dreamed about where I'd go, the adventures I'd have. I hopped on, crashed and quit! How many times does that show up in our lives? We quit after one mistake, one failure. Mary Kay Ash of Mary Kay Cosmetics said: "Fail Forward to Success." People thought she was nuts back in 1963 when she started Mary Kay Cosmetics. It's a multibillion-dollar international corporation today.

One Friday afternoon my First Sergeant comes to my desk and says "Sgt Fernandez, you have the MSF Course and must report to the range at 0800 hours on Monday morning!"

What? No! After my first motorcycle riding experience, I was not looking forward to a second one. I resolved myself to the fact that I had to go. I went home to tell my husband, who says to me: "You are encroaching in a man's world, you belong on the back seat!"

It was at that moment that I realized I was taking a back seat in my own life. I took the MSF course and passed it! That was in 1996, and I've been riding ever since. I have ridden all over Europe, and across much of the U.S., I also made a dirt bike trip across Alaska, the Yukon and the Arctic Circle, raising money for breast cancer research.

My motorcycle is my power and my strength. It's that thing that gives me the courage to go on when I feel like I can't. If I'm having a bad day, I hop on my Harley and take a ride along the coast or find a road with a lot of twisties. I encourage you to take control of the handlebars of your life by hopping in the front seat, taking control of the handlebars and rolling on your throttle to accelerate your success!

— Eldonna Lewis Fernandez, MSgt USAF Retired aka "Pink Biker Chic" rides a 98 Harley Davidson Softail Custom

Meet Eldonna Lewis Fernandez: *She describes herself as a veteran negotiation and contracts expert. She is the author of* Think Like a Negotiator, *and has over 30 years of experience crafting killer deals both stateside and internationally, many in excess of $100 million. She's the CEO of Dynamic Vision International, a specialized consulting and training firm that helps individuals hone negotiation skills, as well as a nationally regarded keynote speaker, session leader and panelist on the Art of Negotiation. Eldonna may be reached online at* www.EldonnaLewisFernandez.com

SO THIS IS FREEDOM...

When I decided to learn to ride a motorcycle, I had two goals in mind: learn to ride and ride as far as you can! I did not make the connection between riding and freedom until I found myself in the middle of the Nevada desert.

My riding story began in September of 2016 when I purchased a 1999 Honda Nighthawk from Craigslist. It was the first step in my journey towards achieving a long-forgotten dream. When I was about ten years old, one afternoon, my older sister and I were busy creating our futures. While she opted for two kids, an economy car and a house, I announced, "When I grow up, I'm gonna buy a motorcycle and ride all over the world!" That memory suddenly came flooding back thirty years later, when I found myself in the middle of an MSF course in the parking lot of a local community college.

I rode my starter bike for ten months, practicing the skills I learned in the MSF course on the streets of Sin City. In July 2017, I purchased my first "big" bike, a 2016 Kawasaki Versys 650LT in candy metallic orange. I named her "Virginia." She spoke to me about her ability to go anywhere--freedom. I liked that.

To me, freedom means the ability to "come and go as you please" or to "live without limits" or restrictions of any kind. These definitions barely scratch the surface of the concept, a notion I would come to realize once I got Virginia up to highway speed on my first ride through the desert.

The Nevada desert is both stunning and mesmerizing. While visually beautiful and frightening, there are many stories about strange things that happen in the desert, alien landings, holes filled with the bodies of wily gangsters and spiritual awakenings. The desert is certainly alive. Amid the tall rocks, black mountains, and cacti, though, I had my first real experience with freedom.

At 65 miles an hour, I was cruising along relishing the fact that I had made a great choice in a motorcycle for my riding style and my future riding aspirations. I felt blessed. Virginia and I were becoming fast friends. She was eating up the curves. The windscreen was doing its job, and although I had begun to feel a little numbness in my throttle hand, I felt good. While taking in the scenery, my mind was busy taking in road conditions, my speed, fuel consumption, and the 70-degree weather. In short, I was doing the "work" of riding and doing my best to "enjoy the ride."

A strange feeling overwhelmed me. This was new. As a rider, I understand the danger that is ever-present on a motorcycle. I understand that few people accept the risk that comes with riding. I had accepted that risk with full knowledge of what could happen. I do this every time I get on my bike. This wasn't a feeling of fear or anxiety. I was no longer worried about my being able to "keep up," maneuvering curves, my speed or the amount of fuel left in my tank. As I glanced around me at the scenery, I suddenly realized that what I was feeling was free.

Riding through the desert among the rocks, I was not afraid. I did not feel lonely, abandoned, or near the brink of certain death. I felt a connection to my bike; it is so much more than just a means of conveyance. I felt a sense of camaraderie with my fellow riders, those in my small group and those I happily waved the lowered "peace" sign to as they passed on the other side of the road. We were all in this together, having the same experience. For a few moments, the world existed, but it existed of my will. I felt that I could change the trajectory of my future with a simple turn down a new road or byway. I could see the road ahead, with its ups and downs, lying straight and curved before me, and on that bike, I felt that I could handle any situation that came my way. Optimism. Freedom.

My thoughts were transported back in time. While the future was ahead of me, I thought about my past and the pasts of women like me. I thought about the trepidation with which I had accepted the challenge of learning to ride a motorcycle. I thought about the many women who were not allowed the privilege of living their dreams. Riding through the desert that day was transcendent. I embodied the spirit of my ancestors, and they were pushing me forward. What did they dream as enslaved Negro women? Would they have accepted the same challenge that I had? What might they have achieved if they had been given the opportunity? Everything. Freedom.

That Saturday afternoon in the desert, I learned a new definition of freedom. Freedom is following your passion. Having the desire and determination to follow your dreams at all cost. The feeling of freedom is riding a motorcycle. I get it now. Fifteen months ago, I bought a motorcycle and learned to ride it. Because I can.

– S. L. Kelly rides a 2016 Kawasaki Versys 650LT.

Meet S. L. Kelly from Nevada. She is a Literature and Composition Professor. In addition to motorcycling, she enjoys reading, listening to music and playing guitar. In her spare time, she can be found in any bookstore café corner guzzling coffee, grading papers and plotting her next move.

FREE WIND THERAPY

"We are strong emotionally, physically, and full of grit, with an iron, will, like the iron horses we ride." - Barb Goodrow

MY BALANCE TO LIVE

After saying I would never ride a motorcycle and being diagnosed with an autoimmune nerve deficiency at 44 years old, I was crippled with pain. I felt my ride in life was coming to an abrupt end at the ripe old age of 47. On the 30th anniversary of our wedding to my school sweetheart, I knew I could not leave without knowing the love of my life would have something to do if I left, so I gave him his dream motorbike, a Modern Classic 2010 Triumph Truxton. I promised him I would ride with him until I could no longer hold on.

Having always been the strong one in charge of my life, after six months of "sitting behind" on our short trips, I decided to go off all medications that made me numb and clumsy and learn to control the nerve pain myself and returned to work. After three years of being a walking, stumbling pill vessel and with the consultation of my doctor, that is what I did.

The funniest thing happened, I decided I wanted to ride on my own. I wanted to feel the wind on my face and have the strength it takes to ride. After three months, I found myself booking into a two-day training session with a wonderful lady trainer. Though I had never actually ridden a motorbike before, I loved it and achieved my license on the second day. I bought my first safe 250 Cruiser a week later. Although I enjoyed every minute, I quickly outgrew it with every weekend ride.

I was not looking for a new bike but went to buy a new pair of gloves and fell in love with the beautiful 650 V-Star

Cruiser that was outside the local bike store. Her name is now "Pearly White" and she is my medication to control my pain and keep my balance. She reminds me that life is too short not to live each day. We have been so many places together and have met so many new interesting people of all ages and walks of life. We joined in so many worthy rides of support that it is impossible to feel alone anymore. I literally ride to remember to live, even my doctor is amazed I have returned to work, made it to age 50 and is mortified I ride an Iron Horse. Our three grown children find it slightly amusing I am a biker now.

– Christeen Werner rides a 2016 Yamaha V-Star 650.

Meet Christeen Werner, she is a wife, mother, and grandmother. She says that she has always lived an interesting life and always worked in traditionally male roles starting as a metal fabricator until studying IT. Christeen became a system network administrator in the 90's, which she has been doing for 20 years. She is currently the Custom Cruiser System Network Administrator in Australia. She has an autoimmune disorder and suffers from peripheral neuropathy of both arms and legs. Despite that, she enjoys many arts and crafts, love horses and supporting her community.

FOR LOVE OF MOTORCYCLES

At the tender age of 16, in the valleys of Connecticut, I was introduced to love and motorcycles, simultaneously. The boy was one who had been in my life since the age of six and stole my heart. Then we lost each other for almost ten years but eventually found each other again.

The motorcycle was a 60's Honda, around 90cc's. Piece-by-piece it fell apart. When the starter went, we ran it down the road and "pop started" it, accomplished by holding in the clutch with the bike in second gear, then after running it along, releasing the clutch, key on of course, and quickly re-engaging the clutch when she sprang to life. I got really good at throwing a leg over, and away I'd go!

As the years passed, the boy stayed, but the bikes changed; 1970's Kawasaki Enduro, 1970's Suzuki 125, then a 1972 Honda 175twin, which I owned for ten years. Never put a dime into her, she ran beautifully, was comfortable and got 60mpg. She was my Golden Girl. During this time, we had our wonderful son. As soon as he could walk, he rode. Napping between us on the king and queen seat as a baby.

I kept that bike, but the man went. I found the bike to be so much more reliable. A few years later, I met man number two, moved to the Northwest Hills of Connecticut and garaged my Golden Girl for several years while I had two more children. When I made the decision to sell her, I took her out of storage, threw on a battery charger, and she fired right up shooting acorns out of the baffled tailpipes! We laughed so hard we cried as the acorns shot out...putt, putt, putt!

When my boys grew some, my original love showed her lovely head once again. As the love-light in the relationship faded, my eye wandered to my oldest son's Harley-Davidson Fatboy and we switched positions, he put Mom on the back.

For years to come I remained a passenger until one day, my son went away for a while, and the Fatboy became mine to care for. For six months she was my little slice of heaven, then I had to give her back.

It was time to do my own thing again, find my freedom, my "Wind Therapy." I found a sweet old Victory, one owner, low miles, well cared for. Traded her for a super-hot Victory Vegas 8ball, faster than the new man's Street Glide, she was super-fast, sleek and sexy.

Unfortunately, in 2012 a young lady texting nailed the rear end of my car and blew out my knee. Surgery ensued. My sexy little beast was traded in on a wonderful Harley Freewheeler, a low slung, high-performance trike, made to answer my prayers.

Riding had been a large part of my life, this little Black Beauty allows me to still tackle the Georgia and North Carolina mountains, the slow, lazy back roads of Florida where I live, and anywhere else I choose to roam. Hu Rah Wind Therapy!
– Laurie Ann Leach currently rides a Harley Freewheeler.

Meet Laurie Ann Leach, she is the owner of Zen Healthy Living for 24 years. A licensed specialist in Shiatsu therapy, hands-on Holistic Healthcare, specializing in cancer care and support. Journey to the Stage, bestselling author, international public speaker and instructor. You can find her at http://zenhealthyliving.wixsite.com/holistichealth

WIND THERAPY

Life as I had known it would never exist again. There are certain things that entails, and the death of your mother was exactly that. Sure I had raised children and grandchildren of my own but are you ever prepared. My outlet was riding. I have ridden since the age of two, posed upon the tank of a Harley Davidson, with my dad. Only now it was mine, and I was riding to clear my head, and my heart. The day of the funeral I packed my bags and headed south from the hills of East Tennessee. Along with my husband, I began the journey. I rode over 400 miles that day and did a lot of reflection and experienced a lot of memories and knew that the best thing for me was the wind. My trip lasted seven days and most of those days were filled with travel and wind therapy. We all handle things differently, but for me, it was my alone time with God and the wind that brought things into focus. Every day of riding is a good day for me with no plans to ever hang up my boots. For every challenge you face riding, you will experience many more rewards. Push yourself, and you will never see any limits! Then you will reach the stars.

– Deborah Stephens rides a 2017 Harley Davidson Road King.

Meet Deborah Stephens. She has been married for almost 38 years. She is a mother and grandmother. Deborah is a semi-retired photographer. She has worked in the construction industry as a pipefitter and welder and was a team truck driver along with her husband for years.

☐

TO SEE THE SUNRISE AGAIN

In the past couple years, I have been fortunate to ride to the Badlands of South Dakota and visit Mount Rushmore. I also traveled south to Tennessee and conquered the infamous Tail of the Dragon and visited country music capital, Nashville. My longest ride in a single day was returning from Tennessee. We stopped somewhere in the middle of Illinois and put in at least 600 miles in a single day to return home. Subconsciously, I must've been preparing for an Iron Butt Run…which is on my bucket list yet to conquer.

My other travels have taken me all across the scenic Upper Peninsula of Michigan and through many towns and cities across the cheese state of Wisconsin.

July 16, 2016 is a Saturday that will be remembered by many that drastically changed my perception of life and just how precious it is. The temperature that day was around mid-80's. It was warm and humid. I was scheduled to have lunch with a good friend of mine but decided to go riding and enjoy the day with my husband. We decided to travel some back-country roads on our way to a local flea market some 75 miles away. Riding back roads on a bright sunny day was not unusual for us, as we try and avoid major highways and traffic. From this point forward, this story becomes somewhat of a vague memory. I mention this now as I have no recollection of the incident I'm about to describe. The details and information to follow were described and told to me by family and friends.

About half an hour into our ride, a deer charged at me from a farmer's field. I flew several feet off my bike, the bike fell over, and my husband who was behind me drove over my bike, flew into the air himself and thankfully landed safely further down the road. I am sad to say the deer did not make it. Apparently, it also had one of my bike blinkers stuck in it. My husband frantically sought out help along a deserted country road. Finally, he was able to seek out someone who immediately called for medical help. I was transported to a local hospital where I resided for approximately three weeks. My injuries consisted of a broken elbow, concussion and an eye injury. A plate had to be planted in my elbow and above my right eye, not to mention a few fractured ribs and plenty of road rash. I was also in a diabetic coma for a couple of days. After all the surgeries were complete, I was then transferred to a rehab facility for an additional three weeks, where my health and injuries were on the mend, and I was finally able to go home permanently before the Labor Day holiday. Mind you, to this day, I have no memory of the accident or my entire time in the hospital or even being transported to the rehab facility. It's bizarre, to say the least, I see photographs of my family and friends with me smiling with them while I was in the hospital. I barely have any recollection of being in the rehab facility. I imagine that someone with Alzheimer's must feel this way. Not a pleasant feeling at all.

Since the accident, I recently purchased my first Harley earlier this year and am lovin' it as much as my other bikes. I am very excited to own a 2011 Harley-Davidson Softail Fatboy, and what a beauty she is. Well, at least I think so. I have never been too particular about my ride. My very first ride was a Yamaha 750, then a Honda Shadow 600, and upgraded to a Kawasaki 800 and then a Kawasaki 900. The brand or model of the bike still does not really matter to me, I just want to ride.

I'm happy to say I rode over 3,000 miles this past summer. It would've been more, but we had quite a few rainy days here. I have another eye surgery scheduled for January which hopefully will clear up my double vision. There are some physical challenges that I'm still working on overcoming, but

I'm taking it one day at a time. I made up my mind after the accident that I was bound and determined to ride again…and here I am...

Today and every day since the accident, or at least from the return of some memories, I count my blessings, appreciate so much more in life and remind myself I am a survivor. I gaze at sunrises and sunsets like there's no tomorrow. A life-changing event such as this certainly opens one's eyes and live one day at a time.

– Lynn Halverson currently rides a 2011 Harley-Davidson Softail Fatboy.

Meet Lynn Halverson, she says she is 49 years young, and we believe her. Lynn has been an avid rider for well over ten years now. She loves riding on two wheels as much as she can. Weather permitting, Lynn usually starts in April and rides through November. She says, "There is no way to describe the feeling one has for that first ride of the year after a long winte"s hibernation."

She currently works in administration for a small company across the river in Wisconsin. Because her job is less than ten miles from where she lives, she rides to and from work every chance she gets. Lynn says, "I probably put more miles on the bike in the summertime than I do my car in the winter."

HELPING ME HEAL

I was hospitalized and placed in a medically-induced coma. While I was in the coma, I passed away twice and no one knew what had made me ill. The hospital figured out that I had pneumonia and had contracted a disease from our organic potting mix particles. Once they had established what they were treating I was on the long hard road back to recovery.

My partner, knowing how much I love to ride, thought he would give some inspiration and encouragement by buying me my first Harley. Previous to that I had only ever had 250cc bikes. In all the time I was in the hospital, he was there every day and thought it would be a good idea to bring me photos of my new bike. I loved it! I could not wait to get home. I was so excited that I discharged myself a little earlier than the hospital would have preferred. I wanted my bike!

Once I got home, I raced out to the backyard to see my legendary Harley. I got to the back door so fast I nearly fell over my own feet. That feeling that I got was like a child getting her first Christmas present.

Jumping, yelling, and screaming, "My bike, my bike I love my bike."

I flung the back door open, and to my surprise, the bike was big, green and had a chopper look. I said to him, "I love you, but you didn't buy it for me." I couldn't even get my leg over to sit on it. It was so large I just wanted to cry.

I'm only 4'10.5" tall and the bike was built for a giant with long legs. That's just not me. After seeing how disappointed still fairly ill I was, he suggested to me that we sell "Kermit" and get me another. He said I could have whatever I wanted. I found another Harley that I thought was the ants pants. I got it home, lowered the front forks, lowered the shockers and changed the seat. The first time I tried to get on it I dropped it. The second time I thought, "Yep I can do this." I picked it out after all. But nope I dropped it again after struggling to ride my bike. I called this one Gurdy. I crashed Gurdy and that was it; I was done. I demanded he sell the bike and that would be the end of my dream.

Low and behold I was invited to a bike party at our local Harley dealer and there she was. I tried the Forty-Eight, then the Iron 883 and thought I was in love. I read all the pamphlets and leaflets and decided not the Iron 883, not the Forty-Eight, not the LowRider, not the Street 500. They just didn't feel quite right. I scoured the pamphlets and found my bike. It's a Harley-Davidson Superlow Sportster. The shortest and lowest bike Harley makes and guess what, he bought it for me. I call her Stella. Now I am learning to control my Stella and trying not to kill myself with the power. It all worked out in the long run. – Jewls currently rides a 2011 Harley-Davidson Superlow Sportster.

Meet Jewls {Julie}. She is 52 and has been riding since she was 14 years old. She lives in a suburb of Adelaide, South Australia. She says that she is living the dream and can't be happier.

RIDING IS MEDICINE FOR THE SOUL

Growing up in a very unhappy home I used the power of visualization as a survival mechanism. I developed a clear picture of what I wanted my life to be like while in the middle of some extremely dark moments. The movie I played in my head was of me in my mid-20's, single, fit, happy, in a nurse's uniform living in a beautiful apartment with a shiny sport bike parked out front. I played this movie in my head daily. Each time it grew in detail down to the furniture in every room.

I was married at 18, became a mother at 20 and divorced at 23. I felt it would be irresponsible for me to ride a motorcycle as a single parent of a small child so I put my dream on hold for another 12 years. I finally bought my first bike. At this point, I was happily married to my love, Milo. Whenever I brought up the idea of learning to ride, Milo would have a meltdown. In 22 years he has only told me "no" to two things. One of those was buying a motorcycle. But being the headstrong woman I am, I figured it would be easier to beg for forgiveness than ask for permission, so I bought one and brought it home in the back of my truck. It was a little Buell Blast I paid $2,200 for and I didn't even know how to start the thing. But like I've done with everything else in my life from learning to drive a stick shift to learning how to become the best strong-woman in the world (yes I owned the title 2x), I figured it out by trial and error. More error than trial.

Luckily, I live in the country and have lots of country roads with no traffic. I dumped the clutch and killed it a hundred times before I ever made it out of my driveway. Two weeks into my journey I got a little overconfident and took a corner with loose gravel too fast and dumped it. I still think that was the best thing that could have happened because I learned how fast a bike can get out from under a rider and I've never

112

forgotten!

When I bought the Buell, I figured I would ride it for a year and by then one of two things would happen. I would either love to ride and upgrade or if I found the bike rarely left the garage, I would just sell it and be over it. Well, the first time I got it up to second gear I knew I was hooked. The adrenaline, sense of freedom, independence, and pride in myself for accomplishing my dream and figuring it out by myself elevated me to emotions words can't express.

Sure enough, a year into riding I sold the Buell. By this time my husband who already had years of riding experience had a bike too. I let him influence me in the selection of my second bike which was totally the wrong bike for a 5'3" woman. I could barely ground my feet, and the Victory V92-SC was too cumbersome, top-heavy, and had a faulty front brake due to the previous owner Jerry-rigging forward controls. I will say that this bike did make me a much better rider. I still don't know how I kept it rubber side down.

A couple years later we ran into hard times so I sold the Victory. Lucky for me a client had a bike rotting in her driveway. She and I bartered $750 worth of services for it, my best buddy got it running and let me tell you, I got every penny out of that Honda Shadow 1100. I rode the wheels off of that bike. In retrospect, I am very fortunate that I never crashed because I was not the safest rider during that time.

In 2011, life had finally leveled out and I was in a situation where I could pick out my very first brand new bike. I had my heart set on a Triumph Thruxton. I felt like I had won the lottery on that first ride home. The bike was so light, agile, and fun it took a bit to adjust to its weightlessness in the corners. I was in love. Red Rocket (as I affectionately called it) and I developed a deep bond over twisting roads, solo adventures, and occasional memories riding with dear friends. We covered 25,000 amazing miles together.

My heart wasn't faithful to Red, though. I had been drooling over the Ducati Diavel but never even considered the possibility of me owning such a bike. I was pushing my little 5-speed 900 ccs to the limit, and I fantasized about what 162 hp would feel like.

On occasion, I would pass the time looking at bikes on Craigslist. One day I spotted a gently used Diavel with only 4,000 miles on it for about 50% off new retail value. I feared it was too good to be true, but I had to take a look. The bike was owned by the type of guy who gets more pleasure dressing a bike up and washing it than actually riding it. It was better than new. By this time I had either broken my husband down or he'd gained confidence in my abilities because he told me to get it if it made me happy. So that's exactly what I did.

I dreamed of taking a long road trip, but the best my crazy life would allow was a 350-mile day trip. This past summer I finally had the opportunity to take a road trip with two of my best friends to Terlingua, Big Bend, and Presidio. I often reflect back on moments from the trip. I will hold on to those memories as some of the best in my life.

Sometimes when I'm riding, I reflect back on my days as an unhappy teen and my dream of freedom, independence, and happiness and I feel the whole emotional spectrum all over again. It's impossible for anyone who has never flown on two wheels through a twisting, flowing mountain pass with the sun smiling down and fresh breeze whipping her hair not to know how wonderfully healing riding is for a bruised and battered soul. It's the best medicine.

– Jill Mills rides a 2011 Ducati Diavel and 2010 Triumph Thruxton.

Meet Jill Mills, *she is a coach and massage therapist in San Antonio, Texas for her company, Jill's Bodymill. She has been interested in health and fitness since she was 14. Jill has traveled the world as a professional strength athlete and won titles such as 2001 and 2002 World's Strongest Woman as well as WPC Powerlifting World Champion. Jill says, "My greatest pleasures in life are my family, my motorcycles, and helping empower other people through fitness." She is happily married with two kids and two grandkids.*

IRON HORSES

"An iron horse is a symbol for women's lives. Transformed by fire into something more, something stronger and free. Mystically, the iron horse represents our individuality while binding our spirits together. When conquered, the iron horse embodies the strength all women possess to face fear and endure. I ride with my tribe." -Sherry Burdick

MY SOUND OF FREEDOM

One of my motorcycle dreams was to buy a cruiser and turn it into a Military Tribute Bike. You see, I served 26 ½ years in the Canadian Military as an Aviation Technician and I felt the need to express myself through that experience. Most of my career was based on fighter aircraft. What better way to embrace my years of service but to display my career on my motorcycle? I was a proud serving member but felt disappointed and unsettled with my "Departing with Dignity" closure. This was my way to resurrect and share my accomplishments as a proud Canadian Veteran. Ironically enough, also an amazing Segway and distraction as I stepped through that undesirable 2012 Christmas gift; my jaw dropping breast cancer diagnosis.

As many can attest, the waiting game for information to present itself plus the inundating appointments can be mind-numbing. Once you start down this road, anything can happen. Finding something to put your brain in is best achieved with something near and dear to your heart. Riding in Canada was out of the question. It was winter and my surgery wasn't slated until February. After that, the undetermined recovery period awaited. I needed to immerse myself in something. Shopping for a motorcycle kept my brain busy and amused most of the time.

Aside from my inquisitive research about my illness, I spent a lot of time reading everything I could to help choose the cruiser I wanted. My chosen chariot was a 2013 Honda Sabre VT1300CS (not available in Canada). The cool, sleek lines and sportiness was my draw to this iron horse. Say what you want, but I'm not a Harley girl. I wanted reliability and It had to have fuel injection, liquid cooling, a shaft drive and ABS brakes. The love affair and bonding began and I spent the rest of the year shopping and dolling her up with countless accessories and accouterments. From front to back, she had a total makeover. Not even the manufacturer would recognize the transformation. The deep throaty sound was amazing when I installed the fuel programmer, added the new air intake and of course the open pipe exhaust. My creation even impressed some of the Harley girls I ride with.

As it turns out, my creation is actually a very comfy ride. My first real long distance test was a trip from Edmonton, Alberta, Canada to Yuma, Arizona, US…1,800 miles and a gas tank that had approximately 150-mile range on it. She wasn't exactly broken-in at that time and I hadn't quite ridden her enough to know how far I could push that range. As luck would have it, I tested that theory and found out by running out of gas just south of Lethbridge. Now pushing my bike to the first house I saw, I realized I was in the middle of nowhere. As I got off the bike in the driveway, I ran into a little guy not quite four years old and cute as a button, dressed in a light jacket, jeans, and rubber boots on the wrong feet. We exchanged hello's and I asked where his mom or dad might be. He took me around the back of his house and there I met up with his dad and little brother working on the deck. I explained my dilemma and asked if he had any gas I could buy from him. Elated to know he had gas, I topped up my tank, paid the man, and I was off again. This time, I decided 100 miles should be my trigger to start scoping out towns and distances to the next gas station. Poor planning on my part but 24 hours in my wake the weather was calling for snow. It was important to keep rolling. Did I mention this trip got a late start, meaning late October?

My trip through Salt Lake City, Utah, was an adventure all by itself. I was following behind a pick-up truck and noticed a desk upside-down bouncing around the box of the truck. The tailgate was down and my first thought was to get as far away as I possibly could. That is an amusing statement for anyone that has ever ridden through the traffic vortex of Salt Lake City. Needless to say, I moved over and as I passed the truck, didn't that desk come crashing out of the back, sliding all over the Interstate. Motioning the driver to get his attention provided nothing in response, so on I rode. When you ride, you see a lot of weird stuff unfolding around you and this was no exception. That four days on the road was my greatest riding achievement at the time. It was certainly the farthest I'd ever ridden. I work a 10/10 schedule at my leisure so I could fly to warmer weather on my days off. The ultimate prize for that accomplishment granted me winter riding in Arizona, hanging with retirees and sharing my crazy plans to paint my bike with anyone that would listen.

I'd been to the Edmonton Motorcycle Show, and an airbrushed trike caught my eye. The passion the owner captured from his military career teared my eyes with the multiple scenes from the war in Afghanistan. The artwork was amazing! That was the reaction I could only hope for with my bike. Through military circles, I eventually ended up talking with the owner of that trike. He (Salty) recommended I use this same artist and told me I would not regret that decision. Some time had passed, but I finally made the call. What a surprise when I told this guy my story and he sounded like he really wanted to paint my bike. I wasn't looking for skulls and flames and I think I surprised him with my request. I wanted airplanes. Specifically, the airplanes I worked on throughout my military career. After several emails, phone calls, and picture exchanges, I tried to provide that perfect snapshot to support my creation. I had no idea where those ideas would take him. I now sensed this guy saw and understood my passion and wanted the opportunity to help me create that one-of-a-kind tribute bike. Now with a motivated artist, I would share a special request. I hadn't shared this with anyone during all of the picture shuffling or stories leading up to this. Since this bike was special and a huge part of my mental recovery, riding or not, I felt the need to have a pink ribbon on it. This would be the humble reminder signifying the loss of my right breast and the underlying inspiration found in the fruits of my labor.

With the collaborating complete, it was time to send the pieces to paint. A day or so of playing in my garage produced nothing more than a frame with wheels. I had removed the front and rear fenders, both side panels, gas tank and my air intake cover. My bike was unrecognizable and now naked. The pieces were then packaged according to Dale's recommendations and sent on a Greyhound bus bound for Manitoba. Once news arrived that the parts made it there safely, there were a few more conversations and picture exchanges. Again, ideas bounced back and forth and as excited as I was, I had no intention to rush him. Deep down I hoped his creative juices would flourish and produce something amazing. Baby steps closer, two years in the making and this project was actually coming to fruition.

Weeks passed and I finally got the long-awaited call. The paintwork was complete. The enthusiasm in his voice reflected his accomplishment and I would be impressed with the outcome. With only the clear-coat finish a few days away he produced pictures of every scene on my parts. You can't buy that emotional experience. Tears filled my eyes when I saw every picture come to life. Every scene touched my heart and took me back to my time in the military. Although he didn't use all my ideas, he captured every aspect of my career and then some.

The now painted parts had returned home to Alberta. The large plastic tote revealed many individual well-wrapped packages. I felt like a kid at Christmas. I was so blessed to have the opportunity to share that opening experience with my parents. They had always supported me throughout my military career and appreciated my excitement and enthusiasm as I revealed my long-awaited treasure. I was not sure of the buy-in my folks had during this entire project but mom's eyes teared as each package opened. A flood of emotion came over me as the pieces were displayed throughout the living room. That shine from the clear-coat gave the pieces a whole new dimension.

It was now time to transform her. While the bike was all apart, I'd installed some ground effects lighting to the frame providing different effects and seven colour choices. I really took my time during this assembly process, ensuring each part was handled with extreme care. My new girl had been resurrected and resuscitated. It was time to present her to the world so others could admire and love her as much as I do. The first show and shine she took every category. Granted it was a small church show, but the response from the public was amazing.

Cancer resulted in a happy ending and has now become a faded memory. The journey doesn't quite end here as the story behind it has evolved. The scenes now presented on my bike tell many tales, and I love to share those stories with inquisitive minds. In my journey, the chapter only ends and new ones present themselves every time I take her out to breathe.

May you all find your own adventure and dream as I present my "Sound of Freedom."

– Terry Lucy rides a 2013 Honda Sabre 1300 and a 2013 Honda Goldwing GL1800

Meet Terry Lucy, *she is a 56-year-old breast cancer survivor and lives in Alberta, Canada. She is a retired military Airframe Technician as of January 2008. Terry now is a Power Engineer, working as a Plant Operator for Imperial Oil North of Fort McMurray, Alberta. She did a lot of trail riding as a kid but didn't get serious until she relocated and bought her first cruiser in 2012. Terry says, "I'm very passionate about riding and have ridden over fifty thousand miles from Yellowknife, NWT to Mexico and West coast to East coast since then."*

OOPS

"Friendship is born at that moment when one person says to another: 'What! You too? I thought I was the only one." — *C.S. Lewis*

SADDLEBAGS NEED TO BE CLOSED

As I have been writing my introductions for different sections, I have become concerned that many of my stories belong in the "Oops" section. I like to remember the fun times and the crazy weather I have had the opportunity to ride in, but the stories that fit in the "Oops" section still make me smile. The smile may be a tad forced, but a smile nonetheless.

About a year after I started riding, I talked my husband into riding from Ohio to Milwaukee for the Harley-Davidson 105th Anniversary party. I had never ridden more than 100 miles in one day so I was scared and nervous. I kept having thoughts about what I would do if I rode halfway there and could not ride any further. We started the morning in the rain and my husband teased me about staying home. We took plenty of breaks so I could stretch and have snacks along the way.

We got close to Chicago and stopped at a gas station for a short break and to fill up. By this time of day, it had started to get warm so I took off some layers. I put a couple of my shirts in my saddlebag and we got back on the highway. We had just started to ride on the interstate that was six lanes of traffic when I looked in my mirror, and I had shirts flying out of my saddlebag, floating down the highway. I very carefully pulled to the side of the interstate and closed my saddlebag that I had forgotten to close when I put my shirts inside. Whenever I tell people about the trip, I always leave out the fact that I forgot to close my saddlebag. But I will never forget the feeling of watching a couple of my favorite shirts get lost on the Chicago interstate. It was so sad it was funny. Feel free to laugh.

– Sarah Andreas

I GET IT HONESTLY

When I told my mom, I was writing this book she said that she would send me a short story to include about the first time she rode a dirt bike with my dad. I told her I would love to include it… A couple of days later this is what she sent me.

A short story about your mom and dad before they were married. I never rode a motorcycle before in my life and your dad was teaching me how to ride. We were riding dirt bikes. It was really fun. We were riding on a dirt drive way on private property. The drive had a wooden road block at the end of it. I did not know there was the road block. Your dad did and he was riding in front of me. When he went around the road block he stopped on the other side of it to wait for me. I was just riding not paying attention. Before I realized what was happening, I rode through the road block and hit your dad. Both bikes and the road block were laying on him. I was in so much shock about what I just did that I just stood there looking at him. Asking if he was "okay". I could not even remove the bikes. Then I started laughing and still could not get myself together enough to move the bikes. It took several minutes to get myself together enough to move the bikes. This is one bike experience I will never forget. – April Kennedy (Sarah's Mom). Now we know why so many of my stories belong in the Oops chapter. -Sarah Andreas

I AM STRONGER THAN MY KICKSTAND

Okay ladies. I wasn't going to write anything because I felt thoroughly embarrassed. But I decided I should tell my stupid little story because I believe it might help someone else out. Let me qualify this story and be clear: I'm a tough girl with good common sense and I'm not so overconfident I push beyond my capabilities. That being said, newbies make mistakes. As some may know, I'm a new rider and haven't taken my class yet. It's coming up in a couple weeks. I've been studying and practicing with experienced bikers who are good teachers. I've had success duck walking, power walking and starting to actually get the hang of the friction zone and brakes enough that I've brought my feet up and done some laps in the parking lot.

Yesterday I parked Cordelia (that's what I call my bike) in my garage head-first. It was my first time turning into my garage and parking. I was pretty pleased with my success. Today, I wanted to turn her around and take a couple pictures of the gorgeous afternoon sunlight. I just put on my new fork bag and swing arm bag so the pictures were a necessity! I duck walked her back and forth and got her just where I wanted her, with her pretty red fender and tank glistening in the sunlight. That's when the mistake happened...I thought I had left my kickstand down, which I had done before, but that was not the case today. Unfortunately, I cannot see my kickstand whether down or up through my floorboard. So as I began to lean her to the left, I suddenly realized there was no support. Immediately, I pushed back trying to right her but her weight prevailed. At least she went down gently onto her engine guard! My leg was well positioned and it was not in any danger.

Here is where the plot thickens: I'm in my garage with the door open. I live in an apartment complex and, of course, other people are coming home from work. I can't close the door

126

because I don't have electricity for lighting. Even so, with the occasional onlooker, I attempted to pick her up. I've watched the videos, understood the technique and began to employ what I learned to no avail. Four times. I failed every single time. Fear and discouragement set in.

"What do I do?"

"I don't have anyone to help me."

"What if I do get her up on the next try and push her too far right and there is no kickstand to catch her?"

I closed the door and went inside my apartment. Deflated. Angry. Frustrated. I wasn't going to call anyone. I was too embarrassed. Then I texted a friend. Too busy to respond. Then I texted another friend. Still at work. My frustration mounted, and I just wanted my baby off her engine guard. I messaged my dear friend who has been teaching me to ride. Initially, I really didn't want to, but I told him what happened and how embarrassed I was. He encouraged me to look up videos and said that I could do it. I said she was too heavy. He said if he could pick up his 900lb bike, I could pick up my Softail Slim.

It took me a little bit, but I listened. I took a few minutes to sit down and breathe. I had my dog beside me as I read the chapter in the *Ride Like a Pro* book regarding picking up bikes. Funny how that was the next chapter I was to read anyway! Even still, my mind was doubting myself. Doubting whether I should be riding a bike at all. Doubting if I have what it takes. Doubting if I am even close to as tough as I think I am. But my friend's words kept ringing in my head, "You can do it."

So, I decided to take one more crack at it. First time: No go. Second time: I got her up about six inches before my hand slipped. Decided my gloves weren't really helping. Took off my gloves and my rings for try #3. Got her up about halfway and my boot slipped a little on my garage floor which is super smooth. BUT I MADE PROGRESS! So then, one last try. I was getting tired but I had the feel of the technique at this point. I pushed, and she began to stand up! I couldn't believe it! I got her up vertical enough but still leaning a bit toward me so as not to go over-center and push too far the other direction, repositioned my body so I could reach the kickstand and put it into position, setting her down on it.

Here is what I learned today: Mistakes happen. Doubts creep in. Dear friends are priceless. And guts and determination win out in the end. Maybe I really do have what it takes to be a Steel Cowgirl!

Maybe those of you who struggle with a little apprehension or doubt can take this away from my experience: Dig those heels in and keep trying. I can't tell you how it felt to overcome something I was convinced I couldn't do myself!!! – Nicole Harris rides a 2014 Harley-Davidson Softail Slim.

Meet Nicole Harris, she is a Licensed Veterinary Technician living in Nebraska. This summer, at age 43, she fulfilled a bucket list item and learned to ride a motorcycle. She and her 2014 Harley-Davidson Softail Slim have 7,600 miles under their belt so far this summer and it's only September. Riding feels as natural as breathing to her. She aims to "live every moment like an angel flies." (Lyric: "Angels in Everything," Blue October)

IRON HORSE, REBEL SOUL, AND GRAVITY

My dream of owning a motorcycle had just come true; I had bought myself the new Harley Davidson XR1200 Sportster. I had grown up riding dirt bikes, how much harder can it be to ride a street bike? Well, I had also grown up riding horses more than dirt bikes and never realized how much that muscle memory would come into play too. After doing a few parking lot runs I knew I really wouldn't get the hang of it till I got on to the real roads, I had a lot of friends that road with a local motorcycle club so I figured I'd be good just riding along with them around town. They were all very supportive of me riding.

So I quickly discovered a problem. I kid you not; I'd come to random stops at stop signs and just fall over. Like a slow-motion movie, I'd stop and just plop right on over before I knew anything! Of course, the guys are laughing, but they came to my rescue and got me up and going. I had no clue what I was doing wrong! A couple of weeks later we went riding again, like clockwork, timber. Plop over we go! Now I'm getting frustrated, mad, and embarrassed. The tips I'm getting are "well you just have to hold it up." What the crap do they think I'm trying to do!

Then came my "Oh" moment. I decide to spend the next day on the horses, something that I can do right. That day the horses were feeling spunky and after a good round of "The Squirrel of Death" a light bulb goes off in my head. One of the main parts of horseback riding that become second nature is to relax and go with the horse. You don't even think about it; I suddenly realize that is what I was doing on the bike. I'd get to a stop, relax and plop right on over! I was able to fix my falling over problem. I'm glad that I didn't give up from the embarrassment and trust me, bikers are not going to pass up telling the next person about the little lady falling dead over from a standstill like a tree. But now it's a story told by the guys in good humor, and I'm laughing right along with them.

Hindsight, I maybe should have started with a smaller bike...

– Stephanie Delong rides a 2009 XR1200.

Meet Stephanie Delong. She describes herself as "a passionate woman when it comes to getting other ladies to ride, I could never put into words what riding has done for me in my life." Stephanie is a 30-year-old single mother of a wonderful seven-year-old boy. They live in beautiful Alabama. Her love for Harleys began in 2008 with her first bike, a 2009 Harley Davidson XR1200. She describes herself to others with the phrase, "I don't have a shoe habit, I have a Harley Habit." She is on her 7th Harley right now and says that she believes she will have this one for a while. Stephanie said, "Ever had that one bike that had the key to your soul? That is when you truly learn to fly." For about ten years now she has worked in emergency medical services and 911 Operations. She says that after everything she has seen and heard, we would think she would have sworn off motorcycles. But Stephanie reports, "Nope, I wouldn't trade getting to see and feel God the way I do on that bike for anything."

MUSCLE MEMORY

I waited for over thirty years to obtain my motorcycle endorsement. After years of scooting around town and on and off of campus on various mopeds, when I finally graduated from college at the age of 48. After graduation, I took the endorsement course and got my license. I had already spent weeks shopping for an 80's era Honda motorcycle. I poked around on Craigslist, public Facebook posts and word of mouth to find just what I wanted. It was only one week after getting my license that I found a 1982 Honda Nighthawk 650 with less than 5000 miles on it in a town about 40 minutes away. I did all the research I could do without actually riding a motorcycle and armed myself with a list of questions and specs to look at when I shopped for this bike. I went by myself to look at it early on a Monday morning. It was beautiful. I fell in love the moment I saw it and knew I was going to buy it if it turned on and ran. It did, I did, and money exchanged hands. I called my son-in-law to help me drive it home later that night. I wanted an experienced rider to drive it home since the only riding experience I had was in the endorsement class. We got it home and pulled it into his driveway. We decided we would leave it at his house so he could give it a more thorough inspection. All I wanted that night was to get on it and ride it down the street and back; I just needed to feel it ride beneath me. This beautiful blue beast was mine, and I wanted to ride it as its new owner. As my daughter and son-in-law watched me closely, ready to critique my every move with that, "just be careful" concern on their faces, I sat on my new bike. I was aware of the scrutiny, and it made my heart pound in my chest, I was so scared of screwing up. I pushed off with my left foot to lift up the kickstand but underestimated the weight of this new machine, and it just kept leaning to the right. I passed the point of no return, and I knew it was going over with me on it. All I could do was fall in the best way I could. There it was - I had just laid down my bike for the first time, and I hadn't even started it yet.

It was intimidating. It was a little humiliating. The story of my fall passed among the family, and I got messages of concern from more people than I care to remember. But, muscle memory is a marvelous thing. I quickly got the hang of the weight of my motorcycle and the only other time I laid it down was when I was moving it in the driveway, and my dogs wrestled their way into my legs as I was kicking down the stand. You CAN do this. You WILL do this if it's what you want. Give it the respect it deserves while giving yourself the respect you need to make it happen. And then keep going.

- Heather V. Irvine. She rides her ride Honda named "Hank". (Read Heather's bio after her Keep your Promises to Yourself story).

MY RAIN SUIT STORY

You know, after you've been riding for a while, you figure out that there is a lesson to be learned on just about every ride. This is the lesson on why you need to purchase a QUALITY rain suit. I don't think I've met anyone who LIKES riding in the rain. It's just part of the experience... You ride, sometimes, you get wet. Well, let me tell you about my very first rain ride.

I was a chilly day in the spring when we left our warm, cozy DRY home to head up to Michigan from Cincinnati. Now, as I said, warm, cozy, DRY home to pull out of the garage in the rain. (I am starting to question my sanity at this point.) Anyway, we leave. In the rain. Well when you ride, you need the appropriate gear, such as rain suit, dry socks, goggles if you use them, full face helmet if you have it, etc. So my husband, (bless his heart – you know you can say anything after "bless your heart" and it's okay) knew I needed a rain suit. (He had a QUALITY one by the way.) Decided that the best one to get is from Dennis Kirk. I think it was one of those $1.99 rain suits. But it was going to keep me dry, so whatever. We take off. I have my NEW goggles, my new rain suit, my waterproof gloves, etc. We meet up with another couple to head north.

Now I haven't been riding that long because I still wasn't a fan of expressways, but to get where you need to be, you sometimes just have to take them. So straight up I-75 in the cold, wet, rain. Let me tell you when you have something new, the best way to try them out is NOT on a 300+ mile ride. But being a "new" long distance rider, I did just that. So I have my goggles, my rain suit, my little self-talks (you can do it, it is just rain, big girl panties, big girl panties, etc.) and I am feeling pretty good about this ride. I am layered-up and for the most part as warm as can be, given the circumstances.

So we hit the highway, and my goggles started squeezing my head. Now mind you, I am the last one of the four in the motorcycle convoy. They are squeezing my head so bad; I thought my head would pop off! So I mess with them, move them around – it's still raining, and it's the only eye protection I have on because I only have a half helmet. So I adjust them and move them and adjust them and move them. At one point I did take them off. By the way, we are going about 75mph up the expressway. I am fidgeting with my goggles, which means, ONLY one hand on the handlebars. Eventually, we stopped at a gas station, and I pulled in looking like Ralphie from the *Christmas Story* movie when he puts his glasses on just after he almost shot his eye out. The other three thought it was hysterical. I was just glad to get them off my head!

We fuel up and off again we go. Luckily it had stopped raining by then, but the further north we went, the colder it got. The rain suit is now another layer that's actually keeping the wind off of me, so I didn't remove it. The ride is going well until all of a sudden my bike STOPS! JUST QUITS! I am on I-75, going 75 (luckily in the slow lane) and my bike stops. I look in the mirror, and there is a semi truck rolling up on my tail, FAST! I get over, off the side of the road and watch the other three continue on their way. I was almost in tears. Eventually, my husband noticed that I was no longer in the back and finally pulled over what seemed to be like five miles away. I had tried to start my bike, but it wouldn't start. I knew I wasn't out of gas because we had just stopped. My husband asked me "Did you turn it off?" Okay, now let's get this straight, WHY in the world, would I just TURN OFF my bike while rolling 75mph on an expressway with a semi on my tail? Playing chicken maybe? My response – "NO! I didn't turn off my bike!" The other two had continued to the next exit, and finally, my husband was able to get my bike started, and we met up with them at the exit. It would still cut out until the day I sold it. My husband thinks it had to do with the emissions.

Off we go again... Rolling up I-75 at 75mph. The further north we went, the colder still it was getting. But the sun was shining, so it wasn't as dreary of a ride. So I'm enjoying it now, and being almost 6 feet tall, I need to stretch out my legs (while going 75 on I-75) and I wiggle around to try to work out numb-butt, etc. Well, as I'm riding, I start feeling something hit my chest, like Tarzan beating his chest in a movie. I was like: "What the hell NOW???" I look down and here, the leg of my $1.99 rain suit had blown out and was beating me in the chest. #%^andand*%# Well the best I can, I stuff the "leg" of my rain suit in my crotch to keep it from beating the crap out of me.

Luckily, there was a dinner stop coming up soon. Oh and by the way, I am no longer the caboose on this train (and I always lead to this day), I am in the middle, so if something unfortunate happens, my husband will have to stop with me – or at least he better! So we stop at Bob Evans for dinner. The other couple was already stopped and off their bikes. My husband and I pull in, and I get off my bike, looking like I just hopped off of an 8-second bull ride with my big ol' ripped to the hip rain suit leg flapping like we were going to have a wild west shootout! God love my husband (bless his heart) tells me not to worry about a thing because he has duct tape and he can fix it! Oh isn't this just my LUCKY day!?

All I have to say is thank goodness that the rest of the trip was uneventful, as I am not sure if I could handle any more issues during that trip. I usually try to find the "good" in everything, but as I said in the beginning, you learn something from every ride. This ride, I learned that I CAN ride in the rain. I learned that you do need a QUALITY rain suit and I learned that I never want to be the caboose on the motorcycle train! – Lori Rosenberger rides a Harley Davidson Street Glide (Read Lori's bio under the Those 5 Little Words story)

NEW BEGINNINGS

In early 2015, I was finalizing my divorce and decided I needed to start living my own kind of life. As part of my bucket list for new beginnings, I included "get motorcycle license" as one of my top goals. In June, I signed up for a beginner course at my local Harley dealership. I fell in love instantly, got my endorsement that following business day and went back to the dealership where my Sporty was waiting for me. Since that day, my entire world has changed.

The second week I had it, I decided to ride to New Braunfels. It was 4th of July weekend. I wanted to feel the warm air and see the fireworks around me. On the way out of town, I ran out of gas. The Sportster doesn't have a fuel gauge, so I had no way to measure what was in there. Fortunately, it was right down the road from a bar. I went there, had a friend meet me and filled it up with gas. Next thing I knew, my battery was dead. Being such a new rider, I was frustrated and had no clue what to do. We decided to hook up jumper cables to the battery. That didn't work. Then, thinking we were defeated, two young bikers stopped and offered help. We ended up becoming good friends. They helped me get a new battery, installed it and that weekend I rode with them on the Twisted Sisters in Medina. It is an experience I will never forget, as well as one that I can laugh about now.

I have put 16,000 miles on my Harley in a 2 1/2 year period. I've ridden to Port Aransas twice, took my friend on the back with me to the ROT rally in Austin, and made many friendships with amazing people along the way. There have been accidents and whoopsies; fortunately though, nothing serious. I hit a whitetail doe once, received the road name "Slider" and dropped it twice while parked in my driveway. I find if you keep your mind and heart aware of your surroundings with a defensive riding attitude, it will help keep you positive and motivated regardless of what happens.

Not only has my life been positively affected, but my son's life has as well. Being only 5 years old, he wants to be just like his mom. He wants his helmet, jacket, boots, gloves and even a tattoo. Being a good role model for him is important to me. I can teach him to have confidence and learn responsibility.

I get told that riding is a "lifestyle," which people state negatively at times. To me, it is a special, freeing experience. I think of it as a way to bond with strangers who are real people as well as a stress management most riders call "wind therapy." One of my favorite things I get from riding is when a little child on the sidewalk sees you, points and waves with a huge smile.

I have inspired many people I know to seek out riding. It is amazing to feel the confidence it will bring. I encourage any woman who is seeking a new adventure and a reason to live to get behind bars.

– Callie Crenwelge rides a 2013 Candy Orange Harley-Davidson Sportster 883.

Meet Callie Crenwelge, she is a 28-year-old single mom. She works full-time as a production supervisor for an artisan chef supply company. She lives in Texas and has only owned one bike which she describes as "a beautiful 2013 Candy Orange Harley Sportster 883."

HIPPIECHICK SOLO TROUBLES IN THE KIMBERLY HEAT

I rode back into Kununurra, had a quick look at an art gallery, looked in the jewelers for the Argyle diamonds then grabbed a sports drink, ice cream and pie to eat before hitting the road. I talked to the visitor center and planned a fuel stop at Doon Doon, Halls Creek, and then Fitzroy. Off I set for Doon Doon. I stopped for a rest about 50km from Kununurra as it was lunchtime, the sun was high, and it was hot. I didn't want to make the same mistake as before with heat stroke so I kept drinking water and lots of electrolytes. I needed to keep riding if I was going to make Fitzroy.

I got about 1km from Doon Doon Roadhouse, and the sign said closed! I thought that was weird because it wasn't Sunday so they must have forgotten to take it down. As I pulled in there wasn't anyone else there, just one utility vehicle (ute). I pulled on the bowsers, but they were locked! I walked around calling out if anyone was there starting to worry. One young tradesman came out, stating the roadhouse was closed. I explained I needed fuel, but he assured me there was no fuel there. I knew it was about 110kms back to Kununurra, so I asked how far to the next fuel, knowing I had about 60kms left in the tank. He explained the next roadhouse was Warmun. I had seen a sign about 1km back saying 92kms! I wouldn't make that. I was stuck. I asked him if he had power tools with four-stroke fuel, I needed a few liters of fuel to make the next fuel stop, but the young worker either wasn't sure or wasn't willing to help, I'm not sure which. I asked if there was anyone else around and his boss came over.

As I was talking with the boss, a tow truck turned up with a construction tipper truck on the back. They were dropping it off as the Doon Doon roadhouse had just been bought by the community there. They were renovating it entirely and that's why they were closed only two days before I got there. The lady at the visitor center must not have known. The boss handed me a 2ltr cold bottle of water, he must have seen how hot I was and sorted out the tow truck. While I was drinking it, I saw a thermometer on the wall. It read 60 degrees C, in the shade. I walked outside with it into the sun on the gravel carpark and towards the roadway, the mercury kept rising, 62, 64, I couldn't watch it. It was bloody hot!

I decided I had two options. One was to buy some fuel from the workers from their jerry cans (who knows if its good fuel or shit), get down the road to Warmun roadhouse for a tank of fuel and by then get to Halls Creek and camp in the caravan park for the night, worried with the motorbike, all my things, and my little tent. Or option two was to ask for a tow to Fitzroy if the towie was heading that way.

Option two may seem like a bad idea, hitching a ride, with a guy I didn't know in the Kimberly's. But of the two it seemed the safer one at the time. So I asked the towie, I offered what money I could afford for the tow, not knowing what it's even worth. He was surprised, looked around and asked who I was traveling with and how I got there not seeing a car anywhere in sight. I explained I was on the bike parked at the pumps; he couldn't believe it. A girl, on her own, with a big motorcycle in the Kimberly's, just before the wet season with no fuel...sounds pretty silly when you say it out loud doesn't it?

He agreed to help me. He was heading to Fitzroy that night but warned me it would take nine hours in the truck so we wouldn't be back until one am. But that was okay with me as I wasn't riding at night. We loaded up the bike, tied it down with massive truck straps and set off after I said thanks to the workers for the cold water and assistance.

The towie was a local guy. His parents were from the

Halls Creek and Fitzroy area. He told me about his travels through South America, and I told him about my travels and why I was traveling now, about how I was trying to get to Port Hedland for the Turtle monitoring volunteer work for my Uni work experience. At Halls Creek he got fuel, and we grabbed food and coffee. I was feeling great, it was easy sitting in the truck, having a friendly chat while enjoying air conditioning. That was the first time in weeks I was feeling cooler. He paid for my snacks for the drive, coffee and dinner, which I thanked him very much for. It was just dark as we hit the road again, there were roos out and many cows as there had been Katherine. We made it safely to Fitzroy, unloaded the bike, and I went to pay him. He refused my money and said he was happy to help. I couldn't believe it! He showed me how to get out of town and down the road to the campgrounds, and where the fuel was in the morning so I could fill up before I left. I couldn't believe the day I had! It felt like a week had passed!

I will never forget how wonderful he was to me, the great chats we had for the drive and the help he offered. It's not every day you meet people like that! Especially in cities. I guess in the rural parts of Australia, it just comes with the territory of being remote. You look after people, but he went above and beyond and I will always be thankful for that. I remember so I can to pass it on!

– Leura "HippieChick" rides a Honda CBR600RR '05 Tuyboy, GSXR750K7, CBR125R (racebike), GSX1400 '08.

Meet Leura, aka Hippiechick started it for a trip she did to Port Hedland for her university work placement unit to work with the sea turtles, but studying meant the expenses of flying and accommodation were too high, so she did a solo ride around Australia for 98 days and under $4k including the repairs to the bike and tires. She has a few blogs from *her travel. She explains that this story was one of the harder days. The others were riding over 1000kms in over 40-degree C heat, getting caught in floods and having to detour 800kms to the Nullarbor. Having to camp around broken hill alone with pig hunting dogs finding her. Plus, she says, "a heap of amazing days like riding 800kms from Port Hedland to Exmouth and swimming at the reef, or staying at Daly waters and meeting amazing other travelers." We can tell she is an adventurer. Her Facebook page for her travels is:* https://www.facebook.com/hippiechick.LK/

JUST RIDE

"Let fear and uncertainty empower you, not overpower you"
-Sarah Fisher

RIDING WITH MY DAUGHTER

My riding started when my dad purchased a mini-bike for us, although my mother was definitely against the idea! I rode that bike and a three-wheeler so extensively that I pretty much wore them out. I remember wiping out on the mini-bike and feeling the pain of the gravel that was embedded in my hands... that I tried unsuccessfully to hide from my mother. The three-wheeler was a close-to-the-ground dune buggy that my dad purchased from the U.S., and somehow, I managed to roll it onto me and was almost killed when a neighbor's gravel truck rounded their bend, and I was driving 30mph right towards it.

Fast-forward to teen years when I was got caught by the police riding the three-wheeler down a back alley in my little hometown in Manitoba. Things settled down when I chose to become a single parent in my 30s and was a student much of the time. I only spent money back then on practical things, until my daughter was having a tough time managing the teenage years, so I asked her if she wanted a scooter or motorbike for her birthday. She just couldn't believe that, out of the blue, for a parent who never spent money unnecessarily, she was able to decide on a red Vespa scooter with a tan leather seat. She loved it and rode it all around town.

I decided a year later to purchase an electric scooter to zip to and from work, but it wasn't really fast enough and seemed to lose juice as soon as it got a bit cold out. So, I upgraded to a Honda Rebel 250. I asked my partner how to drive it, and drove around the block, terrified and almost ran into a ditch. As soon as I took the motorcycle course and drove the bike, I realized that it wasn't quite powerful enough. I then purchased a 650 Suzuki Boulevard. The bike is a perfect size and power for my 5', 106 lb frame. After a few hours of riding, though, the single cylinder seems to wear out my body, so I had purchased a series of other bikes that have never quite fit the same or are too heavy. This year, I bought a Honda CTX, and it's a perfect bike except for the handlebars, and footpegs are just a little too long in the reach. I also own a Honda PCX scooter that I love riding in the city because of its quick acceleration and ease of use in the hilly city of Halifax.

In the meantime, I joined a women's motorcycle club, Atlantic Canada Motor Maids, have made some new friends, and learned so much from these women about bikes and riding. Am thoroughly enjoying their great tidbits of advice, company, and sense of humor. I also helped my daughter upgrade to a 125cc Honda that she absolutely loves for city driving and that fits her frame perfectly.

The best things that I've learned about riding can be summed up as follows:

Take a motorcycle riding course but don't buy a bike until the course is done, and check into common mechanical problems of bikes you're interested in.

In addition, purchase decent gear from the get-go and include a pair of riding pants in addition to the jacket and helmet - if you get the pants shortened, make sure you're sitting down when they measure them!

Finally, research bikes extensively before you even sit on them to see which fit you the best and fits your needs, although, as they say, no one bike will fit every need. For me, the ideal bike would weigh less than 400 lbs, indicate which gear I'm in (I can never seem to remember), includes a fuel gauge, accommodate bags and items for camping, and be able to adjust to my height and leg/arm extension. After these few years of riding, I'm still looking for the exact "right" bike for me, and the only regret I have is not having bought a bike much earlier in life and enjoying the experience (and fuel mileage). I'm looking forward to hopefully many more years of riding, and I think that the ultimate in riding enjoyment will be riding with my daughter if I can convince her to upgrade her bike to a higher capacity for highway driving, and to join Motor Maids! – Pam Pahl, Honda CTX and a Honda PCX scooter

Meet Pam Pahl. She is 52-year old and lives in Halifax, Nova Scotia. She is a single parent of a 23-year old daughter, Rhett Pam is a Personnel Selection Officer and will soon retire from the Canadian Armed Forces. She is a member of the Atlantic Motor Maids. Pam has been riding two and three-wheeled vehicles since childhood. She enjoys motorcycle camping in particular and plans to motorcycle tour a country, perhaps Ireland, to celebrate retirement.

WIND THERAPY IS THE BEST THING EVER!

I used to ride with a local motorcycle club in my hometown, but it was on the back of someone's bike. I got tired of only getting the use of one saddlebag when we went on trips, and always asking someone if I could ride with them. One day I put a bid in on a 2005 Victory Vegas and won! Now I was committed to ride. When the bike arrived, I was so excited. But nervous also. I had never ridden a bike before, and it was a pretty big one to start with.

I took the riding course in 2006 and passed. I was 43 years old. In November of 2015, I loaded up my bike and spent the winter with my parents in Arizona. I met some girls who were with the Women in the Wind Cactus Cuties Chapter. I rode all winter with them, and they became my sisters. When I came home in the spring, I started a Women in the Wind chapter called the Red River Valley Chapter. We now have 22 members in our chapter with everyone having different levels of riding experiences. Last summer I rode with a friend to South Carolina, riding through 9 states and the Tail of the Dragon!,
– Becki Jacobson rides a Victory Vegas.

Meet Becki Jacobson from Minnesota. She has been riding for 12 years now. She did not start riding until the age of 41. She is now retired due to health problems.

MOTORCYCLE & MISFITS COMMUNITY

You know those streaks on the rear windows of all parent's cars? I am just about convinced those are from little kids like me who couldn't get close enough to those iron horses running down the road just out of reach. Growing up my parents fielded ceaseless questions about motorcycles, and handled hours of pleading for my very own "iron horsie." Year after year birthday wishes fell on deaf ears, the sharp words of "donor-cycle" spitting out like venom anytime a family member heard my wistful ramblings. I can't blame my parents for trying like hell to instill the fear of god in me about motorcycles. They did their best, albeit they still failed miserably.

It all started in a strange place, one would think; when I was 18 I became gravely ill. I was hospitalized with a severe blood infection known as sepsis. My organs began to deteriorate and to put it lightly, I damn near didn't make it out of that white, sterile ward. When I finally did, it took a year to be able to function remotely like a human again. Luxuries such as jogging, running, and dancing that I had used liberally prior were now a faint memory that would fade even more over the years. My heart and orthostatic systems were severely damaged while I was sick, I as a result have a severe Mitral valve prolapse and something called P.O.T.S. Which is basically a myriad of problems that resulted in me being pretty well up shits creek for an 18 year old. I became isolated, introverted, and felt overwhelmingly useless. Things start looking up I promise.

Wistfully browsing Craigslist motorcycle adds was a time sink that brought me the ability to day-dream of something that made the corners of my lips upturn and my stomach flit about. Checking every morning looking at things that were elegant and at the same time so raffish. Reminiscing of those days spent with my nose pressed against the glass, only worry in the world was that the beautiful flying machine was slowly getting away. One morning a tilt shift in my life occurred in the form of a rather poorly written Craigslist add for a rummage sale at a local motorcycle co-op. I skimmed it, and closed my computer

I'd hear that bike startup and leave at the same time every day. That sound created a goal. That rumble, that putt, lodged thoughts that represented strength and freedom. The thought of learning to ride gave me a huge ambition to recover. I knew I needed to be strong mentally and especially physically if I wanted to ever handle a motorcycle. With that determination, my recovery was in motion.

Motorcycling feeds my soul unconditionally, and literally, has saved my life. I am now a published poet, freelance writer and above all I'm content with who I am.

I believe so many women who, like me, need this self-actualization in one way or another. Women who are on the edge and need a healthy outlet are now seeing other women ride and have decided to take this on. The ride is whatever the universe has in store. With that, inspire and motivate other women to get outside their comfort zone, and feel strength and power from within.

Riding my motorcycle is absolutely euphoric. It's an ecstasy that expands perception and understanding on so many levels and delivers us into a life time of camaraderie and good times. It's hard to share that emotion and feeling with somebody who hasn't experienced it. It's the ultimate freedom and I try to connect that feeling through my writing. I want women who ride, or are on the fence to learn to ride, to feel what I feel. Poetry through riding has given me an opportunity. Motorcycling really is an elevation. I could have the worst day ever and once I get on my bike, I check out of those thoughts and into new visions. The day's problems seem to fly off in the wind and whatever is weighing me down is not very heavy anymore. It's this sort of magic, a connection you have with something greater than yourself.

– America Salvatore rides a 2017 Harley Davidson Dyna

LowRider named "Daughter."

Meet America Salvatore, *she is a native of Brooklyn, New York who now resides in Southern California. She is a freelance writer, poet and animal activist. America lives with her husband Max and dog Chazz.*

A LOVE FOR MOTORCYCLES THAT FILLS MY HEART

It was a chilly fall afternoon in September 2014 when I opened the mailbox and got the surprise of a lifetime. There it was, my photo on the front cover of *American Motorcyclist* Magazine, wearing a crisp white professional suit, holding my helmet, and proudly standing next to my KTM 300 XCW in the center of the UMBC college campus with the number plate 334. While I had recently been interviewed by the American Motorcyclist Association (AMA) for a piece they were writing called, "Unlikely Riders," it was beyond my wildest dreams to imagine they would put me on the front cover and share my story with thousands of readers.

As a mother of three, a Girl Scout leader, and a university administrator with a Ph.D., who did not start racing competitively until the ripe age of thirty-four, I could not fathom why I was so deserving of this honor, especially since speed and skill were not on my side. In fact, I had never even won a race and barely knew anything about competitive racing. Even though I had rode a dirt bike since I was six years old growing up in rural West Virginia, I was still an amateur by all respects and had much lingo to learn like, "roosted," "holeshot," "harescramble," and "brapp."

I'll never forget my very first race just one year earlier at the Blue Diamond MX Park in Delaware, where I showed up to the line surrounded by nearly 300 men with no clue about what I was getting myself into. My husband Ryan was very supportive and tried to calm my nerves but as "ten seconds" was announced, I immediately questioned if I had lost my mind. The idea of quitting was not far-fetched, however, by this point it was too late to turn back. Before I knew it, I was riding a wheelie off the start line, not intentionally of course, twisting the throttle as if my life depended upon it, and weary about what obstacles might be looming ahead. After three brutal laps involving roots, ruts, tight woods sections, a staircase, and one broken toe later, I proudly finished the race in second to last place.

Even though I felt a sense of achievement and had conquered a major fear, I wasn't a hundred percent convinced that I was cut out for competitive racing. However, any notion of doubt quickly faded when I met two fierce competitors, Kelli Gandy Silvers and Patti Lloyd Blair, both of whom I learned were grandmothers also trying their shot at competitive racing and who instantly gained my complete admiration and respect. For whatever reason, maybe fate, I met these determined women at a critical decision point. Kelli and Patti were brimming with "sportswomanship" and eager to welcome me into the East Coast Enduro Association (ECEA) family, which was exactly the kind of reassurance that I needed in that moment. Fast-forward one year, exactly ten races later, and there I am standing at the mailbox holding the *American Motorcyclist* Magazine with my picture gracing the front cover.

In complete disbelief, I flipped through the magazine and read the several page spread called, "Changing Perceptions: Everyday Motorcyclists Buck Popular Notions." Within days of national release, I began receiving a steady stream of emails, letters, and phone calls from fathers, mothers, young girls, and many others who felt, in some way, inspired by my story. I couldn't help but to feel a sense of pride that the words on those pages were positively received, and in some cases, offered just the amount of encouragement that was needed for complete strangers to try riding a motorcycle for the very first time.

One of my favorite emails was one that I received from a fellow female rider, 2011 American Motorcyclist of the Year, and champion of Dirt Bike Girl Adventures, Nancy Sabater.

Little did I know at the time, but this new found friendship with Nancy and other racers like Samantha Kilgore and Heidi Hawkins was the beginning of something much greater, much more powerful. It was the beginning of a sisterhood that would grow exponentially over the years as I met more and more women alike.

As I reflect upon the incredible moto journey that I have had since riding a Honda 70 as a little girl at age six, to entering my first ECEA harescramble race at the age of 34, to landing the front cover of the *American Motorcyclist* Magazine, I am overwhelmed with gratitude. It is however, the sisterhood that has been gained through it all, one that is bonded by a common passion and a love for motorcycles that fills my heart most and feeds my soul.

– Amanda Marie Knapp, KTM 300 XCW

Meet Amanda Knapp. She has been passionate about riding motorcycles since she was a little girl growing up in rural West Virginia. When Amanda was six years old she got her first dirt bike – a Honda 70 and has been shattering misconceived notions about female riders ever since.

While Amanda primarily competes in the East Coast Enduro Association (ECEA) Harescramble Series she has also tested her skills at the Kenda Full Gas Sprint Enduro, the Northeast 24 Hour Challenge and participates in local events and charity rides as an active member of the Green Marble Enduro Riders (GMER). Professionally, Amanda is a university administrator with a Ph.D., who has blended a career in higher education with off-road motorcycle racing to help students, "stay on track." Amanda is has been featured in numerous publications for her efforts in "changing perceptions," "outracing stereotypes" and "pushing past obstacles."

https://academicpolicy.umbc.edu/appointment/

CAUGHT MY SPIRIT

My bike story begins before February 22, 1978, but I feel like I caught my spirit on that special day. That was the day I turned 12 years old. For many years I had been begging my parents for either a mini-bike or a horse. My dad is a former farmer always said he would not be getting a "grain burner" on his ground. It was on that cold winter day in 1978 that my parents took me into our living room to receive my birthday gift. Now February in Ohio is not exactly the ideal time to receive a mini-bike, especially that year, as it was the year Ohio had a blizzard. Perhaps that is why my parents brought the bike into the living room. My greatest wish had been granted, and I was the proud recipient of a 1977 Honda XL75. It was so shiny and had the wind on the Honda emblem on the tank and chrome on the wheels and turn signals. I spent many hours riding in our yard with neighborhood boys and up and down our dead-end street. As I got a little older, I was allowed to venture into other neighborhoods. We also built ramps made from one to two cinder blocks and a board. We had to make sure the board was arranged just right so it didn't smack up behind you as you made the jump. These were the days of Evil Kenevil, and we were acting the part. There was also a boy in the neighborhood whose dad worked for Honda. He dad was higher up with the company and would often bring home bikes that were going to be released. I remember them by having a yellow Honda and trying the Honda Odyssey when it was still a prototype. In my mind, it was a magical time of innocence to grow up. Time moved on, and I got my driver's license leaving behind my Honda XL75. My dad traded it for a go car for my brothers because he feared they would be too crazy on the bike and would get hurt. *Go figure!*

Twenty-eight years later my husband purchased a 1998 Kawasaki KLR650. I told him I wanted to take it for a ride. He questioned my ability, but I reminded him I had ridden a lot when I was a kid. So, with hesitation, my husband helped me get on the bike. You see it was a bit of a challenge as I am only 5'2" and the KLR is a pretty stout dual sport bike. Getting on that bike took me right back to my youth. I was 12 years old again, and all was well with the world. I should have known better but later that week when my husband was at work I hopped on his bike and attempted to take it for a ride. Long story short I dropped the bike taking my left knee out tearing my ACL. I had to have surgery to repair the ACL to return to my busy job as an Emergency Room nurse. Even with my injury, my spirit had been awakened, and I wanted to ride. My husband decided it would be best for me to have my own bike, so he purchased a Honda XLR 250. I got my learner's permit. I finally got the courage to take the test for my motorcycle endorsement. I am now riding a Honda Shadow 750 and looking at possibly getting another bike. Perhaps the next bike will be a sport-touring bike if I can find one for my short stature. I have to thank my parents first for unveiling my spirit with that Honda XL75 and then my husband for purchasing the Honda XLR 250. Riding is the best thing ever, and I love meeting other women who also ride. Remember you are never too old to try something new. I am now a 50-year-old grandmother, and I have slain the "Dragon" US Route 129. I look forward to many more years of adventures on my two wheels.

− Chris Kuhn rides a Honda Shadow 750

Meet Chris Kuhn, she also lives in Ohio. Chris told me that she listens to the Misfits on her 60-mile drive to Westerville, Ohio where she works as an Emergency Dept. nurse at Mount Carmel Saint Ann's. That is where she heard about the call for submissions for this book. Chris says that she has seen her share of tragic outcomes with motorcycle accidents, but it has not deterred her from riding. "There is something about riding that just gives you your spirit. If you would ever like to meet up for a ride let me know. I am always up for a new adventure!"

BREAKING STEREOTYPES

There are always two reactions I get when I am riding my motorcycle:

1. When I have my helmet and gear on I get called Sir A LOT. There is always this embarrassed pause when I remove my helmet or speak, and they figure out I am not a sir.

2. The next question is usually, do you have a death wish? I think stereotypes are to be expected because I don't know that

many women who choose to ride their bike, and there seems to be this stigma out there that all bikers, are drunk, dirty, and just asking to die on their bikes. I blame part of this on the hit new TV series *Sons of Anarchy* I would like to offer up some contradiction to these reactions and tell you a little about myself in the process.

I have been riding a motorcycle of some kind since I was 12 years old. My parents introduced us kids to bikes at an early age. My first bike was a Yamaha 125 TTL, I don't remember the year, but my parents got two on some sale, and I remembered thinking how cool they were, and we learned to ride in the dirt lots around our house in Beautiful Butte, Montana. There were two rules: 1) always wear your gear; and 2) never run from the cops... There was already one Evel Knievel in Butte; the cops didn't need to worry about us, too!

As I got older, my bikes slowly got bigger and less dirt capable. In college, I rode a Suzuki DR200 to class every day there wasn't snow on the ground, and frequently got ticketed for parking on the lawn of the chemistry-biology building at Montana Tech. For those of you unfamiliar with Tech, there are like 600 stairs to get from the parking lot to class, and I was usually running late. (The bike fit nicely on the little cement pad for parking pedal bikes.) I traded the DR for a Honda Rebel as I have always wanted my own road bike, and the DR just didn't cut it on the highway. Well, the Rebel had this scary death wobble that started up around 60mph, so I rode it around town and to work and school for a few years. I just couldn't afford much in the way of a motorcycle with school and life going on.

After college graduation, I moved from Montana to Wyoming to pursue my dream job as a Fish Culturist. The Rebel stayed behind in my dad's garage. There was no town to ride it in, and it was too scary to ride on the highway. I missed it, but after three years of sitting, it was time to move it. I sold the Rebel. That was the first time since I was 12 that I never had a motorcycle. It was awful.

I have always wanted a classic Indian motorcycle, you know the kind, that bike you find in someone's barn and spend 15 years getting it to run. Well turns out those are hard to find now. I dug around all over Wyoming, Idaho, and Montana looking for one, to no avail.

The very next year Polaris released their new line of Indian Scouts, they were touted as the best bike for small people. I am 5'3" and have a heck of a time touching the ground on some of the road bikes on the market, that's why I never got one, because I really don't have a death wish. I want to be focused on the bike and the road, not my inability to stop because I can't reach the ground. But life had caught me again, and I had just spent a whole bunch of money on my wedding, and honeymoon to Alaska. I couldn't possibly afford a motorcycle now.

Funny thing about life is there is always some obstacle preventing you from doing what you want. You have two choices: let it keep you down, or work harder to get around whatever obstacle is in your way. It seems I am always taking the 2nd option. I worked my butt off, got a part-time job in addition to my career, saved my money, paid off my debt, and wouldn't you know, I had that 2016 Indian Scout parked in my garage the next spring.

To all those new lady riders out there, motorcycling is one of the best ways I have found to instill self-confidence, to keep your mind and body sharp, and to meet new people. I recently joined the women's motorcycling group, the Motor Maids, and I cannot wait to see what the future holds for my riding career! Not all bikers are drunk, dirty, and asking to die on their bikes, in fact, the majority of people I have ever encountered on a motorcycle are sober, friendly, and very safety conscious. I work hard every time I ride to be courteous to others, mindful and safe while driving, and I NEVER drink alcohol and ride. I try very hard to attend at least one training class a year, and I am always looking for a riding partner!

Some ladies ride, but they can be few and far between, especially in Montana, where the riding season is extremely short. But if riding with others is important to you, there are plenty of groups out there to ride with, and most men are helpful and supportive of women riders. I mostly ride with my brothers and husband. But if you can ride with other women, DO IT! Taking that first step to my first ladies run two years ago was some of the most fun on a motorcycle I have ever had.

I am back in Montana now, and my husband and I are saving for bike number 2. It turns out he likes riding just as much as me, but not on the back. But that ladies, is a story for another day! Get the bike, get the safety gear, training and ride that sucker until the wheels fall off!

– Kerrie Berger rides her 2016 Indian Scout.

Meet Kerrie Berger, she is 28 years old and from Montana. She is married to Brian, and they have three dogs. She has a Bachelors Degree in Biological Sciences. In her career, Kerrie is a Fish Culturist.

THE WIND IN YOUR HAIR

My motorcycle story began when my sister-in-law asked me if I wanted to take the MSF course and get our licenses since our husbands both had motorcycles. I was a game and went, without any intention of getting my own motorcycle. My first day of riding on the little bikes, I was having a bit of trouble and thought, "maybe this isn't a good idea!" I even asked the guy next to me if I was making him nervous. Then suddenly it all clicked, and I got the hang of it, and then I was thinking, "What am I doing on the back?", and that was it; two weeks later I got my first bike, a 2009 Sportster 1200 low. I put 40,000 miles on her in 5 years and then traded her in for my current bike, a grey Fatboy Low, which I totally love. I have been riding since October 2010 and never looked back.

After obtaining my motorcycle license, I joined a women's riding group and fell in love riding with women. I enjoy riding with my husband, but riding with the girls is a different ride. Since then I have become a member of Stilettos on Steel, a women's riding group based in Wisconsin. I brought SOS to NYS in April of 2016, and we currently have 45 members throughout New York. We often get our chapters together and have done an overnight excursion out in the middle of nowhere with the cows, renting a house and thoroughly enjoying one another's company. I have been on many long distance trips with women riders as well as with my husband. I often put at least 8,000 miles per year on my bike – and that is in New York alone. I have ridden twice over to Tennessee to ride the Tail of the Dragon; once with the ladies and once with my husband. The longest distance riding was with my husband. We went to the Tail of the Dragon and stayed the night right there at Deals Gap. I highly recommend staying there, it's inexpensive, and the atmosphere is wonderful, the camaraderie with other bikers from all over the country, even outside the country, the conversation and the enjoyment of bikers as one was a wonderful experience. The connection was palpable. After the Dragon, we went all the way across North Carolina to the coast at the Outer Banks, then up the coast to Chincoteague, through Pennsylvania and the Poconos before going back home.

Since 2010, we have gone on our vacations on our motorcycles, and I wouldn't have it any other way now. My vest bears memories from most of the places we have traveled. Being an independent woman rider has made such an impact on my life, on my confidence, on my enjoyment of life. It's one of the best decisions I have ever made. I took a risk, took the chance, and have never looked back! I have had some close calls on my bike involving cars that apparently did not see me, and a close call with a deer. I saw that deer's big black eyes, heard its hooves clacking on the street trying to miss me, and all I could do was slightly lean to the right to try and avoid it, which I was lucky enough to do, and as I looked in my rearview mirror, I saw the deer fall onto the ground; it did all it could not to get hit by me – thank goodness. The freedom my bike affords me when I'm riding is beyond description, the experience hard to explain. Think back to when you first rode your bicycle as a kid, the wind in your hair, the freedom, the speed, the fun. To me, riding takes me back to that magical time as a kid; that wonderful feeling of freedom as you fly down the road on two wheels. It's a feeling you just can't beat.

– Fayne Winter, rides the Grey Goddess a Fatboy Low

Meet Fayne Winter; she is 55 years old. Fayne got her motorcycle license when she was 48. She lives in New York. She is married, and has two children and one grandchild - all boys! Fayne tells us her motorcycle nickname is Bugsy, and her Fatboy Low's name is the Grey Goddess.

IF I AM RIDING, I AM HAVING FUN

My first memory of Harley-Davidson is from when I was five years old. I was standing on the sidewalk with my older cousin waiting to cross the street when a group of motorcycles rode past. I remember the hair standing up on my arms as I asked my cousin what that was. He said, "Harley-Davidson motorcycles."

I thought to myself at that moment that I had to have one of those one day. It took 42 years for that dream to come true, and my life changed completely when I purchased my first Harley.

I did not grow up around bikes and had never been on one when a friend came to me in December of 2006 and asked me if I wanted to buy his bike. I was six years clean and sober through the program of Alcoholics Anonymous. I had met some sober bikers and they had what I wanted. One friend in particular was a man I had gone to high school with. We called him "Reverend Booger" and he was instrumental in making my long-time dream come true. He, along with many other sober bikers, took me under their wings and patiently taught me how to ride.

I bought my Sportster in January 2007 and it sat in my garage until March of that year. I enrolled in a Safety Course early March and failed the course. One of the instructors told me, "If I were you, I'd never get on a bike again."

Thankfully, I had some great Brothers and Sisters who kept encouraging me to never give up. I was terrified but I persisted in a routine of getting to know the bike. At first, I got on the bike, put it in neutral and walked it up and down my driveway until it was comfortable. Then I started the engine and with it still in neutral, I walked it up and down my driveway. When I was okay with that, I started putting it in gear, going up and down my driveway. This is how I started.

One day in April, Booger called to invite me to a meeting of the sober bikers group and he told me to ride to his house and attend the meeting. This was the first time I had had the bike out of the driveway, but I did it! I rode the 15 or so miles over to his house and I was hooked. The next day, I rode to work and I have been riding ever since. I have ridden with this group as a member since July 2007. There are chapters of this group all over the world, and I have been able to ride with hundreds of men and women to numerous events hosted by the group.

My first long trip was in July 2008. I rode an iron-butt from Georgia to Wisconsin and then on to Canada and Niagara Falls. Booger, Hitch and I rode over 3,000 miles that week, and it remains the most memorable trip I have ever taken. That year, I won the mileage contest our group held with 30,679 miles clocked on my Sporty for 2008. Also that year, when I had only been riding about six weeks, the group invited me to ride The Tail of The Dragon, a curvy mountain road in Tennessee made up of 312 curves in just 11 miles! It was exhilarating!

As we were preparing for our annual trip to Wisconsin in 2009, our Friend and Brother, Reverend Booger, passed away suddenly. It was a horrible time for all who knew him. At that time, I was driving a big rig all over the country. Our group, with chapters everywhere, was very kind to me and provided me with bikes to ride whenever I was in their towns and had downtime in my truck. That year, I rode a chopper, an UltraGlide, a Honda VTZ 1300, a Softtail with 18" apes and an old Shovelhead, just to name a few. I gave up driving a truck in September of 2009. I had to give up my Sportster that year as well, so 2009 was a year of mixed emotions to say the least. I ended that year owning a little Hugger.

It was early in 2010 when I acquired my current bike, a 2002 Dyna Superglide. This bike was previously owned by my Brother, Booger. After his passing, his wife came to me and said she wanted the bike to continue being ridden as Booger rode, every day. That's how I came to own this bike. When I got it, it had 93,000 miles on it. Today, it is coming up on 158,000. It is not a shiny bike...it is a workhorse, and I ride it as such. Booger would always say, "The Dyna was made to be ridden, not polished!" I carry on that legacy to this day.

I am a self-proclaimed EDR, Every-Day-Rider. I have no idea how to "winterize" a bike as mine rarely sits for more than a few days at a time. I have been known to ride 200 miles South to meet with folks and ride 400 miles North. My motto for riding is always, "I 'wanna go!!"

I ride with two Muppets, Kermit and Animal, strapped to the sissy bar of the bike. There is a story behind that too. Every time Booger would take off on a trip, his wife, the Caretaker, would insist he take Animal along with him for security. Kermit represents Hitch, who rode with Booger and me in 2008 to Canada. The two have become permanent fixtures on my bike. I also have a 5-year-old Jackahuahua (part Jack Russell, part Chihuahua) named Rita who rides with me in her own little carrier.

I can't imagine where I would be in my life had I not started riding when I did. Riding is such a huge part of who I am today. I have had so many women (and men, for that matter) who want to talk to me about riding, wishing they could ride, and I always say to them, "Just do it! If I can learn to ride, anyone can!" Ride on, Sisters and Brothers! It's a wild ride, and I wouldn't take anything in the world for my experiences in the wind!

– Debbie "RahRah" Ezell, rides a 2002 Harley-Davidson Dyna

SuperGlide.

Meet RahRah, she is a school bus driver in Walker County, Georgia. Her first bike was a 2006 Harley-Davidson Sportster 883 which she bought in January 2007. Today, she rides a 2002 Harley-Davidson Dyna SuperGlide. She has owned this bike since 2011. Rita, RahRah's little dog rides with her a lot, along with the Muppets that are always on the back of her bike. She lives in an area where she can ride year-round, and she does. In fact, she rides almost every day unless it is raining, snowing or below 20 degrees outside. There are only a handful of these days each year where she lives.

BAD ASS RIDER

I had been riding behind my husband was for about 10 years until one day I decided I wanted to be upfront in control. So we borrowed a dirt bike from a friend and I learned in our backyard going around in a big circle. I learned the basics and it was a pop-start so every time I tried to start it, it would pop back and hit my leg so I had a big bruise on my leg. But I was determined to ride. My husband paid for my class which I passed on the first try while riding a Suzuki 250. When my husband took a Harley-Davidson Sportster 1200 custom in on trade, I went from the dirt bike and the Suzuki 250 to the Sportster.

This bike was a bit bigger so just to get the feel of it I would put it in 1st gear, go to the end of my drive still in 1st and back it up then repeat. My driveway is only about 20 feet long and overall I put almost three miles on my bike just from doing that. Then I kept it in storage in town and when we got off work, we would go to a lot so I could learn to ride it. Even when I passed the test, I was still riding in the lot. Until one day I asked myself why I was doing that.

I decided to take it to the streets and rode my Sportster 1200 for about 7 years. Some people would ask:

"How can you ride that?"

"Doesn't beat you up being a hardtail?"

But that bike worked for me and I guess I knew no different from anything else. It was fine and comfortable for me. I didn't have a windshield so I decided to step up to a bigger bike. I decided on a 2014 Softail Slim and I fell in love with it. While riding my Sportster, I had a vision of what my next bike would look like and I bought the Slim in June 2014. But I didn't get it until August because of all the custom work I had done to it. It was like my vision came to life. It was a big WOW.

Now I still ride with no windshield or fairing. I must be a bit old school because I don't like the looks of them and I get a lot of respect from the men and women for riding like that.

I just took a trip to Texas. It was an attempt to set a world record of women riders in one location. We didn't break it, but I did ride by myself to Texas from Missouri. While going there I was trying to do an Iron Butt run, but with the rain, it slowed me down. I didn't get it. I just missed by about three hours. But I did ride over 500 miles in the rain by the time I reached Bandera, Texas. I was beyond very wet...I was dripping wet. While there, I decided to ride the Twisted Sisters in Texas. That was fun so all together on that trip I rode a little over 2,300 miles round trip and had a blast. Now that I did that and because I ride by myself without a windshield or fairing, a lot of people say I'm a Bad Ass Rider!

– Brenda Chapman rides a 2014 Harley-Davidson Softail Slim

customized to her vision.

Meet Brenda Chapman, *she just turned 50 in September. She lives in Missouri. Brenda is a Private Caregiver for a 90-year-young woman and has been with her for six years but all together has been an in-home services provider for about 15 years.*

"THE FUN TRACK" OR TEARS AND SNOT!

My name is Kathy and I'm a Rebel (better than being an alcoholic I guess). In 2007 I got my tattoo done at 42 years old. This was an "I left you after 18 years, and now I will do as I damn well please" tattoo. That same year I applied for my motorbike learner's license. My son had his bike license and I thought "How hard could it possibly be?"

My 16-year-old son rode my brand new Honda CBR125 home and then the fight began. There were tears and snot. Why couldn't I get the damn bike up the driveway and who the hell came up with the bright idea of having a clutch on a handlebar?

"My son could ride, spat it!"

After two days, he was no longer prepared to tolerate my abuse of him and the bike. He signed me up online to do my learner's license the following weekend. Onwards and upwards was an understatement. Once I had the basics down pat, I was off and I loved it!

In 2009, I met Mr. Wonderful. By this stage I had a new bike, a brand new lovely red Triumph Daytona 675. Eventually Mr. Wonderful and I became an item. We liked a lot of the same things but also liked to do individual things. Riding to us was not an individual thing; we did it as a team. He has many years riding experience and I had a lot to learn from him.

"LET'S DO THE OODNADATTA TRACK," he said, "IT WILL BE FUN," he said.

To do this said "fun" trip, I bought a Suzuki DR650 road/trail. With only one month of dirt road experience he took me on a local track that he said would be fun. Not only did I crash the bike on this "fun" track, but I got muddy and it sucked! I was quickly learning that his idea of fun was entirely different than mine! This also made me wonder how much "fun" this Oodnadatta track was going to be.

We rode from Hobart in Tasmania to the start of this "fun" track in the middle of Australia. This track is 600km's long. It's rough and corrugated with many dry but very sandy creek beds and we were told to pray it doesn't rain. Riding on it was like riding on marbles...for 600KMs! The first 200km's I took it easy, nothing over 60Kph and I'm sure it was driving Mr. Wonderful crazy as he was chugging along at 90-100Kph and kept coming back as I was so far behind.

We had a lovely camp for the night and took off again at first light. This was because I took so long the day before. I guess he figured it was going to be a very, very long day. At the 300km mark, I had had enough! Mr. Wonderful rode beside me, and I STOPPED! There were tears and snot and lots of expletives. I think at one point I even told him to get me a helicopter and get me the hell off that track! Well, Mr. Wonderful being as calm as he is, rode off! Not a word, just casually rode away.

PFFT!!!! He'll come back said I, as his dust was getting smaller and smaller. Yep, he'll be back aaaany minute now. By this stage, there was no dust. And then it dawned on me, HE'S LEFT ME! I cried even more, the tracks red dust was now a soggy, muddy mess running down my neck.

The realization of this was that I was going to have to go the 100km to Oodnadatta just so I could get a bed for the night because Mr. Wonderful had the tent! Then I was bawling again at that thought. So I started the bike, the trusty dirty DR650, and off I went. 20 km's later around a corner I rode, and there was Mr. Wonderful waiting for me. He came over and gives me a cuddle and asks if I was okay. *Seriously?* If he could have seen in my visor the disgusting mess I was, he would not have asked that. Anyhow, I appreciated him asking.

I wasn't quite sure what to do though. He said all he

wanted me to do was stop crying. YES, I was still crying 20km's later! We got to Oodnadatta and had a great night's sleep. I actually really enjoyed the final 200k's of that "fun" track, but nothing beats seeing that bitumen and stopping one meter onto it and kissing it!! Yes, Mr. Wonderful took a picture of me doing that. This track was just a small part of the 17,000km's we did on a six-week trip around the middle and west of Australia.

Would I do the track again? Hell yes! Would I make another road trip on the bikes again? Hell yes!

Did this make me stronger? Absolutely! I was very proud of being out there having a go at it at my age.

Did this cement the bond between Mr. Wonderful and me? You betcha!! We have been a team in most everything we have done since then. I hope someone got a giggle out of my story, we laugh heaps about it now. Keep riding Ladies, Keep Smiling, and enjoy the moment! xx

– Kathy Ballard rides a DR650.

Meet Kathy Ballard, she lives in Tasmania, Australia. She currently works as an executive P.A. She still has her trusty DR650 from this story...his name is Jack...as in, Jack of all trades!

WHO WILL I RIDE WITH?

"My iron horse makes me feel like I am a force to be reckoned with and a beacon onto others who dare to dream to ride the wind." -Melissa Wild

WE DO WHAT WE LOVE

I started riding when I was 12 years old, mini-bikes and go-carts mostly. I enjoy riding immensely. When I got older, I seemed to always date guys who rode. That's how I met my (ex) husband. He bought my brother's motorcycle. We rode a lot. When we got divorced, the riding stopped. A friend encouraged me to get my license, get a bike, and go ride myself. SO THAT'S WHAT I DID!

I rode with my brother's crew (all men at the time). Then one day I met a woman who had a Women in the Wind patch. I asked her about it, looked them up, and attended a meeting. That is when my riding really took off.

After riding with my brothers and their crews, I definitely think riding with women is a totally different kind of riding experience. We don't care how big your bike is, or how loud or fast your bike can go. We don't bar hop, we do what we love, we RIDE. We have women who have traveled across the country on solo trips, women who have done 1,000 miles in a two-day span, and women who have encouraged other women to dare what they have only dreamed of doing, get their licenses and their own bikes and ride.

Now I ride with the Wharton, New Jersey American Legion Riders, Post 91. And I am one of six of the founding members of the NJ Renegades chapter of Women in the Wind. Our mission is to unite women motorcyclists with friends of common interest, to promote a positive image to the public of women on motorcycles and to educate members on motorcycle safety and maintenance. There are four founding members left. We have assembled a great group of women. Sisters you can ride with, confide in and be yourself with.

I remember when I first started out riding, women riding wasn't common. I was never one to fit into a mold of what society says women should be or do. You should do what you love doing. Riding has taken me out of my comfort zone. It has made me a more confident outspoken woman. And the friendships that I have made with my Renegades sisters are priceless. It is a sisterhood and bond that will last a lifetime. I am very lucky to be able to ride with them and share experiences both on the road and in life. I am not sure what else to say except follow your dreams, don't let anything stand in your way.

– Melissa Wild rides a 2016 1200 Harley Davidson Sportster.

Meet Melissa Wild, she is a single 59-year-old woman with two amazing kids Kaleigh and Will (adults actually). Melissa says, "Their spouses are a great addition to our family, my awesome son-in-law, Steve and my new daughter-in-law Laura, and two handsome grandsons, Steven and Jaxen (to date - hoping for more!)" She has two fur babies, Beau and Bella. She has worked as a legal secretary for the past 28 years. She tells us, "I ride as much as I can, and if I can't ride, I find myself occupying my time with woodworking projects, cooking, or hanging with family and friends. But riding, that is the most gratifying for me. It keeps my head clear, keeps me focused and keeps a smile on my face! It has taken me to places I wouldn't have traveled to, and I have met people I probably wouldn't have met if I wasn't riding. Who could ask for more than that?"

FACING FEARS

Six years ago, I was a naïve rider with more passion than experience. I was riding an automatic scooter in Northern Thailand (where I live) on a gravely pot-hole ridden road. At one point I thought the road was in better condition, so I picked up speed, to my folly. I turned a corner and I landed straight into a large pothole. My scooter went one way and I went the other. I remember none of it due to a concussion. My riding partner was the one to tell me what happened when I regained consciousness. I sustained many injuries, particularly on my face, as I was wearing an open-faced helmet. I feel lucky to be alive and lucky to have a face left. In fact, I recovered remarkably well.

This is not a tale of woe though, it is a tale of triumph.

In the six years since my accident, I have battled to improve my riding skillset both mentally and physically. I pushed myself to face fears. It was slow progress initially, but my love of riding and desire for adventure spurred me on.

One of the first realizations was that I needed to be riding a manual bike. Next, I needed to buy a decent bike. I bought a Kawasaki Dtracker 250cc. This was three years ago, which is when the adventures really began for me. Soon after buying the Dtracker I bought a GoPro camera and began documenting my rides. A couple of years ago I began blogging about my trips. To my surprise, I gained followers.

Since that accident I have clocked up quite a few KM's, covering a lot of ground, usually solo, around Thailand regions. I ride mainly rural areas, border regions and restricted access zones. I like the technical tight twisties and unpredictable curves.

I took dirt bike training to get over my fear of falling. A healthy fear of course, but it was a fear that was affecting me too much. So I learned to fall. I learned how to tackle gravel and dirt and control my bike.

I recently returned from taking my bike over the border into Northern Laos. The road conditions in Laos are much more unpredictable than Thailand roads but I loved it. I felt confident and able. I met wonderful people and children that touched my heart.

When I reflect upon today (for, as I write this, it is exactly six years ago that I had the accident), I feel proud of my achievements. Since this date, I have connected with amazing riders internationally, both male and female, and made some great friends. I started a Facebook group for lady riders in Thailand which has helped link Thailand-based lady riders of all nationalities to connect with inspiring lady riders in the region. I have participated in a number of charity rides such as The Distinguished Gentleman's Ride and local charity events. I like who I have become. I also know that many more adventures lay ahead. I will always feel a sense of sadness about the accident, but it has also brought many positive elements. I used to hesitate, doubt myself, and not live up to my full potential. Now I seize opportunities. Having nearly lost my life, I now live it to its full potential. I can honestly say that I am now very much alive.

– Zed CM rides a Kawasaki Dtracker 250cc.

Meet Zed CM, she is originally from a small town in Scotland, but she has lived in several countries from a young age. For the last 11 years, she has been based in Chiang Mai, Thailand. She began riding in Thailand around eight or nine years ago on a 115cc automatic scooter, then upgraded to a 250cc manual bike. She has explored around Thailand regions (and recently Laos). Zed is a professional blogger and writes a motorcycle blog and creates videos and guides about riding in Thailand. Here is a link to her blog: www.motogirlthailand.com

MY FIRST LEATHER AND LACE MC MEMORIAL RUN

It was March 2010, and I was a prospect attending my first Leather and Lace MC Memorial Run. It became a run forever burned into my memory, and I have not missed one since.

It started on a beautiful, clear sunny morning. All the sisters had completed their bike checks in preparation for the day's event. The Road Captain gathered us together and gave the safety brief. She explained where we were going, what we would be doing, along with the what if's, and what to do's. My sponsor had already explained to me the meaning of the memorial run, so I knew it was going to be something special, but I had no idea just how special this run would end up being for me. I understood the run was to remember our Sisters in Heaven, that they are forever a part of our lives, always with us in spirit no matter where the road takes us.

Once the Road Captain brief was over, it was time to line up our bikes, all full patches to the front with our National President, Jennifer Chaffin, leading the way. As a prospect, I was near the back of the pack with the other prospects. It did not matter where I rode in the pack as I was honored and proud to ride with my club sisters, following wherever the President and our Road Captain took us. I could tell this was an important run by the actions of every full patch in the formation. I cannot find the words to describe the emotion I saw on their faces.

The Road Captain gave the mount up sign, and our President fired up her old school Softail, quickly followed by the rest of the bikes. The sound put a big smile on my face, caused my heart to quicken and goose bumps to appear. Before I knew it, we were ripping down US-1, one long pack of bikers who happen to be women, riding side by side. It was truly a sight to see and something amazing to be part of.

I remember seeing other bikers and people stuck in cages staring at us as we passed, many taking pictures and waving, some even turning around to follow us from a distance. I also remember the complete unity I felt as we rolled together as one, as sisters, with precision and discipline. I remember thinking about the sisters that came before me, some not with us anymore, and some still leading the way, each one has paved the road for me to ride free.

As the pack rolled through some long sweepers, I was able to get a clear picture of our National President out front. I thought about her leadership, dedication, loyalty, and love for us all. Her commitment to the club's vision had not waivered for 27 years!

About that time, I began thinking more deeply about our Heavenly Sisters and how I wished I had known them. We are told many stories of these wonderful women, and I could tell how much they were missed in the words of our older sisters. We also have an area in our clubhouse where we can sit quietly to reflect and read about them, look at their pictures, all in honor and in keeping with the promise that we will never forget a Lace Sister. All of this flashed through my mind, and I began to feel a sense of solemnness. I was overwhelmed with emotions, not something I usually wear on my sleeve. What was this feeling? Oh God, I don't want the full patches to see me like this, suck it up, prospect!

The hand signal came back for the pack to turn into a park located on the river. We pulled in, pulled up, shut our bikes down, and backed next to each other into the parking spaces. Once we got off our bikes, we took group pictures, some talked about our Heavenly Sisters, while others stood quietly by the river. We stayed as long as needed, comforting each other, full patches checking on the prospects to make sure we were doing okay. That is when I noticed their emotions, and I knew then they had me figured out. I realized it was okay to have feelings and show them, that I would not be judged or ridiculed. These full patch sisters, some who barely knew me, understood and had my back. I felt like I had known these women all my life. They got me, and I got them. Even though we were different in many ways, we were more alike than I ever realized. Before I knew it, the Road Captain gave the mount up sign, as it was time to get rolling again.

The feelings I had as we headed out were not as solemn. I felt a sense of connection to the full patches and an eagerness to learn as much as I could from them. I fell in love with my club. I knew I wanted more and these women, my sisters, were going to teach me the right way.

Before we returned to the clubhouse, we stopped for lunch at a local restaurant. Breaking bread with your sisters is a very special time. We had a chance to learn more about each other and our love for riding motorcycles and helping children. The bonds I developed are for a lifetime. Even today breaking bread with my sisters is special, a time that nourishes my soul. Soon it was time to pay our checks and begin the track back to the clubhouse, a place we call Home.

As much as I didn't want the run to end, I looked forward to getting back to our clubhouse. I wanted to hear more stories about our club from the full patches. It was a time spent learning our history, traditions, and proper protocols. It was also a time of laughter, love, and more bonding.

My first Memorial run was unforgettable for me in so

many ways. Each year that I make this run, I still get a big smile on my face, my heart still quickens, and goosebumps still appear. I still get emotional thinking about our Heavenly Sisters, and I do not care who sees it.

Fast-forward to 2017; our club will celebrate 35 years in March of 2018. The success of our longevity rides with our leaders and the sisters who dedicate themselves to the club and its vision. I am riding at the front of the pack now, and it is my turn to mentor our prospects. It is my turn to show the prospects it is okay to let go and be who you are and not fear judgment. It is my turn to share stories of the Heavenly Sisters I knew. It is my turn to show them I have their backs no matter what. We have a saying in our club that we are our sister's keeper, and our actions are proof that we really are. I'm sure our Heavenly Sisters up above are smiling down on us all.

– Debora "Boots" Lewis rides a 1973 FLH and a 2007 FLHX.

__Meet Debora Lewis.__ She is the National Sergeant at Arms for Leather and Lace MC. Boots retired as a 1stSgt from the United States Marine Corps. She joined directly out of high school in 1976 and proudly served for 20 years. She was a member of the USMC Rifle/Pistol team early in her career and is a combat veteran of Desert Shield/Storm. The Marines showed her the world as a motor transport chief and competitive shooter, but her two tours as a drill instructor were the most rewarding. Immediately on retirement from the Marine Corps, Burton Fire and Rescue hired her as a full-time Firefighter/EMT. She earned a degree in Fire Science Technology, served 20 years retiring as a Battalion Chief. A biker of 43 years, she joined Leather and Lace MC in 2009. She enjoys riding her motorcycles, hanging with her club Sisters, marksmanship, golf, and relaxing at home with her family.

SEEING NORTH AMERICA ON THREE WHEELS

I started riding at the age of 55, and I haven't stopped. I have ridden in Indiana, Ohio, West Virginia, Kentucky, Pennsylvania, New Jersey, New York, Tennessee, Arkansas, Missouri, Illinois, Wisconsin, Iowa, Michigan, Oklahoma, Texas, New Mexico, and Ontario, Canada.

My first bike was a 750 Honda Shadow; I took a lot of falls while I was learning to ride, I even hit my co-workers car, an embarrassing moment for me. I started to ride on outings with my son and daughter-in-law, Jason and Sarah Lee, daughter and son-in-law Tonya and Ron Anderson, and their friends. Watching these experienced riders I was able to learn a lot, they were very patient with me and helped me to become a better rider.

I joined a group of riders in my hometown, and we helped to raise money for our Veterans in the area. The group went a different direction, and I left to ride with the Patriot Guards, and I still participate with the flag lines for our fallen veterans. Riding with the Patriot Guard I met a woman named Sugar (Margarette Menges), she kept telling me about a group of women who were long distance riders, after six months of speaking with Sugar, I finally met some of the lady riders for dinner. The women belong to the longest women's riding club in Northern America. This club is for long distance riding and has been in existence for 77 years, and they are called Motor Maids. They have members in all the states and Canada.

My first year riding with the Motor Maids I put 10,000 miles on my bike, this year I rode over 13,000 miles. Every state has events, and all Motor Maids are welcome to join the fun, but you have to ride your bike, I try to make the other states events as often as I can. The Motor Maids have a convention every year, and you meet women from all over the United States and Canada. I have laid my head to rest at so many different Motor Maids home. They always welcome you anytime. There have been many times that I met these wonderful women for the first when they offered me a place to sleep and a meal.

I want women to know that no matter what age you are, you can learn to ride a bike and meet wonderful women on every adventure you take. So, take the motorcycle class, buy a bike and see the world, it will be the best time of your life. — Mary Lee-Kanyuh rides a Honda 1800 Goldwing, with the California Side Car Trike

Meet Mary Lee-Kanyuh, she is 63 years old and happily retired. Mary has two children, who she raised as a single parent, and two granddaughters. She has lived in Indiana for 39 years. For a long time, she did Obedience Trials with her standard poodle, Sami. But when Sami, passed away, Mary's interest went in a different direction. She decided to learn to ride a motorcycle, and she is still riding to this day.

PARADE OF SISTERS

I left East Texas in hot, clear weather, expecting a four-hour ride to San Antonio. I made it to Seguin, on the east side of San Antonio, and chose the rest area there to stretch my legs and call my son. I asked him about the weather, to which he cheerily replied, "no rain since this morning." I climbed back on the bike and headed west.

The horizon had the wrong color. No thunderheads, just a gray blanket covering the horizon of the mission city. Within 15 minutes I was riding into a deluge. Reaching the first exit, I found covered parking at a service station. I yanked my two-piece rain suit out, pulled the britches on over my leather boots, and zipped the jacket up and away I went.

Within 10 minutes, I felt the first rivulet running UNDER my rain suit. Then I distinctly felt water running down my torso. Water is running inside my legs and down inside my boots. Water is splashing off my chest and up under my full-face helmet. I was sitting in a buffeting car wash of rain. The water level inside my boots had filled, and each time I changed gears, the rainwater moved up and down my calf. I kept my visor squeegeed off with the back of my hand, and determined my windshield was worthless in a downpour. My layers of clothes were saturated and stuck to me under the rain gear. Water ran off my eyelashes, under my visor. The exit I had memorized finally approached, and I safely arrived at my son's home. My beautiful boots were placed in the bathtub to drain. I applied warm clothes to my exterior, and whiskey on ice to my interior and called it a day.

It rained all night. I wrapped my second pair of leather boots in bags, put nitrile gloves over my leather gloves, removed the windshield and left before sunrise. I kept my speed slow to keep from hydroplaning. I reached Bandera and headed to the city park to join my fellow women riders for our Ride with the Mayor. Sisters were under the pavilion, looking just like me. We all had wet hair, wet clothes, hot coffee and our stories of travel binding us.

Our ride took us into the Texas Hill Country, the curviest and most beautiful roads of Texas. Known as "Twisted Sisters," it is notorious for many motorcyclist deaths. We were heading into this, in the rain. Our leader let us know to ride at our own speed. Something I noticed quickly was the smell; the scent was of juniper and fresh water. It was wonderful. We rode through a unique area of maple trees that canopied the road, called Lost

Maples. We traveled across low water crossings and snaked out way around hairpin turns and elevation changes. Our rally made it to Leakey, where we stopped at a motorcycle shop and grill. We peeled wet layers of gear and ate a hot lunch, sharing stories of our lives. I sat at a table full of women that rode in from Tampa, Florida. Two of them were cancer survivors. One woman had spent the summer traversing the country on her Harley. After group pictures, we took off in the rain and headed back to rally headquarters, then split up to find a dry place to land.

During the night, the week-long deluge ceased, and we awoke to blue skies! It was Saturday, and the official Parade of Sisters rally ride was this morning. We were trying to break the world record of women riders in one event. I rode into town, with my son following. He had started on his first motorcycle at the age of five on a Honda 50cc. He was thoroughly enjoying riding with his 55-year-old mom. We rode all around town, showing off my custom bobber, very dirty and much ridden. Old country Texas cowboys were waving at us, along with leather dressed bikers. As I made my slow ride into the park, women started whooping and yelling over the rat rod bobber. I revved throttle and yelled back. It was intoxicating. It was a rush. It was entertaining. This is what a beauty pageant must feel like. We hollered, yelled and my bike did her loud BRAAAPPPP of approval. It was women on bikes as far as I could see. I staged behind two sisters that rode in from Iowa. A spectacular Indian motorcycle pulled up beside me. It was a full dresser, cream and bluebonnet blue paint with tan, fringed bags. We exchanged names and admired each other's rides. Twin sisters from Kansas riding matching Harley trikes staged behind us. They climbed off their trikes, and I discovered them to be maybe five feet tall, in their 60's and full of sass. We discovered the Dallas Litas ahead of us. One woman came through looking for Chrome Angels. I met sisters from Iowa that had ridden down. We watched a drone launch overhead to cover our huge rally from the sky. Armbands with an official count finally were passed out, and mine was #684. We finally started the rally ride through downtown Bandera, and it was awesome. Throughout the entire city, people packed in to cheer us on. They were screaming approval of my bobber, and I would twist her throttle releasing her loud BRAAAAPPPP. We made a slow ride into the guest ranch and parked, then congratulated each other and praised God for the beautiful weather.

I headed back to Houston in perfect riding weather. The ride back was at a slower pace, and I enjoyed the country roads of Texas. The last hour before reaching home was making my ass ache. I was showing 1,300 miles. My fingertips had blood blistered; I had mystery bruises, sunburnt flesh, a terribly twisted pile of helmet hair, dry eyeballs and I could not have been happier.

— Kerrie Kerns rides a 2008 Harley Davidson Softail Crossbones Bobber

Meet Kerrie Kerns. She purchased her first bike after caring for her dad until he passed. She said that grief consumed her, and she just wanted to run away. But being a sensible person, she says she did the next best thing which was to buy a Harley and start riding. Kerrie said, "Dad was cremated, so I carry a beautiful cobalt blue bottle with his ashes on all my trips. I love riding solo and exploring our beautiful country."

THE BEGINNING

Many stories conclude with The End… this one is The Beginning. Riding motorcycles becomes part of your DNA. I hope that you enjoyed reading the stories as much as I enjoyed collecting them for this book. I have to admit that sharing more than just my riding adventures and stories was a lot of fun. I truly enjoyed the connection that I built with each of the contributors. I have made many new friends who I hope to meet in person over the next couple of years. These women are amazing! Their support, cheering and generosity is more than what I was looking for when I came up with the book's subtitle: Rebel Souls, Golden Hearts and Iron Horses. Each woman who contributed to this book reflected these traits and filled me with gratitude and honor to be able to represent them in this way.

I hope that their stories have inspired you to Embrace the Journey!

Sarah Andreas

MEET THE AUTHOR

Sarah Andreas has worked in the motorcycle industry for more than 12 years. Riding a Harley-Davidson motorcycle is one of her favorite summer pastimes. Sarah lives on a 250+ acre farm in Strasburg, Ohio, with her husband Dan and their son Marcus. Yes, she knows how to drive a tractor and ride a Harley-Davidson motorcycle!

When she is not riding her motorcycle, Sarah is an author, speaker and coach. As the founder of WiseWood LLC, she shares that her purpose in life is to teach, research, coach and write about leadership development.

Sarah has a Master of Business Administration degree and is currently doing her dissertation work for her Ph.D. in Organizational Leadership from Johnson University. A lifelong learner, Sarah is a Kent State Certified Lean Six Sigma Black Belt, a Project Management Professional (PMP), and a DISC® Facilitator. She uses these skills to help her clients identify their current state, future state, and develop a strategy plan to move forward on their career journey.

Her first book, Career Advancement Strategies for Emerging Leaders, was released in 2016. It was written to help young professionals discover simple things that could hold them back in their career.

Sarah often shares an African Proverb: "If you want to go fast, go alone, if you want to go far, go together." Sarah believes that by building and maintaining relationships we can create growth and development for everyone. It is this belief that started Sarah on the journey to write *Women Who Ride*.

You can contact Sarah via email at sarah@wisewoodllc.com

MEET THE EDITOR

Nicki Snyder served as the copyeditor for this book, as well as Sarah Andreas' first book "Career Advancement Strategies for Emerging Leaders." Nicki is 33 years old, has a Bachelor's Degree in Communication Arts with a focus in Journalism, and has a passion for anything involving words. She loves reading, writing, editing, athletics and adventure, and has 10 years experience working as a Marketing Director in the motorcycle industry. She works full time as a director in marketing, social media, public relations and advertising. She got her motorcycle endorsement in 2008 and fell in love with the sport of motorcycling immediately. She lives in Dover, Ohio with her husband, Cory and three sons; 6-year-old twins Braxton and Braylon and 2-year-old Landon, who keep her on her toes. Nicki is working on a number of personal projects including her personal fashion blog and 2 additional book concepts as well as editing.

"I absolutely love editing and this was by far my favorite project I have ever worked on," said Nicki. "Sarah is a longtime friend of mine and this piece turned out beautifully. The words and stories of these women are inspiring, exciting, motivating, and so diverse. I laughed, I cried, and had goosebumps more than once while reading these contributors' stories. My favorite part about the sport of motorcycling is that it doesn't matter who you are or where you come from, when you're out on the open road, everyone is equal. Ride on and keep rockin' ladies!"

More contact information:
Email: nickisnyder@gmail.com
Facebook: Nicki Rottman Snyder at
https://www.facebook.com/nickisnyder
Blog:
https://www.fashionforwardmomfashionbackwardbudget.wordpress.com

CALL FOR SUBMISSIONS TO BE PUBLISHED!

Women Who Ride -2019

Stories and Tributes to the Women who have Rebel Souls, Golden Hearts, and Iron Horses

BOOK SUBMISSION IDEAS:

Inspiration and experiences from learning to ride, finding the courage to start the process, riding across country, friendship, oops... I forgot to put the kickstand down, left my key on and the battery is dead, I dropped my bike, how I overcame my biggest fear related to riding, starting riding after 30, 40, 50+, motherhood and riding a motorcycle, friendship, marriage and relationships, and life, promotion, work/ride balance, and any other topics of interest to inspire a new Rebel Soul.

DEADLINE: October 5, 2018. Up to 1,000 words per submission, plus 50-75 words of your Bio, with name, profession, city, states, and bike(s) you ride! Email in a text message or Word.doc file to: author@womenwhoridebook.com Indicate "Book Submission" in the subject line.

INCLUDE:
• Your suggested submission title.
• Your name, the make/model of your motorcycle and title to be printed with your contribution.
• Your contact name, email, phone.
• Name of publication, if your submission has been previously published.
• Indicate that you have permission to reprint if your work is previously published.

RELEASE DATE: January 2019! Website: womenwhoridebook.com
FB Page: https://www.facebook.com/womenwhoridebook/

COPYRIGHT: Original stories, quotations and tributes remain the property and copyright of the contributor. NO FEE to participate in this publication. NO OBLIGATION to purchase printed books. NO royalties are given for selections accepted. Books are published through: WiseWood, LLC.